Come Home
to *Comfort*

Bringing Hope, Happiness, and
Harmony to Today's Busy Woman

Sharon Hoffman

New Leaf Press

First printing: February 2003

ISBN: 0-89221-544-5
Library of Congress Number: 2002116493

Printed in the United States of America.

Please visit our website for other great titles:
www.newleafpress.net

For information regarding author interviews, please contact
the publicity department at (870) 438-5288.

Dedication

To my mother
Lindy Baird
in whose heart and home I find sweet comfort!

Thank you.

Blessed be God. . . . Who comforteth us in all our tribulation, that we may be able to comfort them which are in any trouble, by the comfort wherewith we ourselves are comforted of God (2 Cor. 1:3–4).

They shall not hurt nor destroy in all my holy mountain: for the earth shall be full of the knowledge of the Lord, as the waters cover the sea (Isa. 11:9).

And he is before all things, and by him all things consist (Col. 1:17).

SHARON HOFFMAN is a much-in-demand speaker because of her engaging manner, wit, and warmth. She is the founder and director of GIFTed Living, and has been involved in ministry with her husband, Rob, for 30 years. She lives in North Carolina and is the mother of two married daughters. She has one granddaughter.

Acknowledgments

My heart holds dear all the precious ones in my life who have helped to make these pages a reality . . . many thanks from my heart go out:

To my husband, Rob, for giving me daily gifts of love, encouragement, and perspective. The greatest comfort in my life is having you by my side!

To Mindy and Rick, Missy and Mike — how grateful I am to be your mom. You bring chaos and comfort to my life . . . I love both!

To Dana Grimes for your polished writing contribution, and especially for your sustaining prayer, perseverance, and *pushing.* (You always seem to know when I need the latter!)

To my dear CCBC gals for carving out periods of quiet for me and for being an awesome "test group" for much of this material. Your lives verify God's comfort!

To the New Leaf Press family! You heard my passion and have been great each step of this project. I'm grateful to partner with such a godly, fun-loving team.

To Florence Littauer for your enthusiasm right from the start! You and Marita truly *wanted* me to write this series. You're the best!

To Marabel Morgan, whose teachings when I was just a newlywed spawned much of my learning for loving my husband and my home.

And to you, dear reader friend, may God truly be the comfort of your heart and of your home.

Introduction

Welcome. I'd love to invite you into my home through the pages of this book. One of the greatest benefits of having a home office nowadays is the flexibility to do just that. I delight in the break that a spontaneous visit with a friend brings. So, go ahead; make yourself right at home. Feel free to dog-ear or highlight a few pages as you're reading. You won't find perfection. For certain you won't see a superhero. What you will discover is an amazing journey of how our home, as well as my heart, has been through many stages of rebuilding and restoration. You see, God has taken me on quite an adventure in order to construct His loving comfort into my life. He had a beautiful design for my life and for my home — far more wonderful than I could ever have dared to imagine.

How about you? Is your home ready for some improvement projects? Let's take a look at it in some new and exciting ways. You may live in humble quarters of a rented room or apartment or an itty-bitty cottage. Perhaps the place you call home is a sprawling three-story, Victorian manor or maybe a sprawling suburban ranch. Wherever you call home, if you want your home to survive, yes truly thrive . . . then this book is for you!

You may be not unlike the friends I have met in recent years through an avalanche of correspondence and while speaking in conferences across the country. Do you know what I find? I find, indeed, that the number-one common denominator in every corner of the planet is the precious place we call *home*. The heart-cry of women of every age and every season of life is still that of nurturing a place of comfort. These pages are lovingly composed to help you do just that. Get ready to dramatically change your life, because God has a marvelous ability of taking the ordinary and turning it into the extraordinary. You might be surprised when you find where we'll start. More surprises will follow when you discover where touring through your home will take us.

Dear reader, you may be thinking, *My home doesn't have a prayer.* If so, I encourage you to stay with me. I used to think the very same thing, but I've witnessed some remarkable turnarounds. You can, too. I urge you to make another try. Every house (and the people living in it) needs a few home improvement projects from time to time. Remember, "Rome wasn't built in a day." And neither is a home!

Go ahead; snuggle into the plump pillows on my sofa. That's what they're there for. I hope as you enter my home through reading, you will feel the laid-back coziness that my family and I take pleasure in when we're at home. We'll share a cup of tea, cocoa, or coffee — your choice. It is my prayer that you will hear my heart. These pages are lovingly composed to help you discover truths that can transform your home from a place of chaos into a haven of comfort. God alone is the true comforter. This is a book about Him and His abundant happiness, hope, and harmony. How do I know these things to be true? I opened the door and invited Christ in . . . and my home is living proof.

Come Home to Happiness

Entering a Home of Joy

By the time my husband, Rob, and I made the down payment on our home, I had lived in about as many houses as I was years old. When I was a child and throughout my first few years of marriage, we moved often. A home of my own represented a "putting down of roots" — which would be an important element in my quest for personal comfort and stability.

The moment our realtor and I first stepped inside our home-to-be, how my heart sank! Walking through each room confirmed the harsh reality of what I'd suspected from the outside. The whole house was in dire need of *major* repair and remodeling. Yet the minute I walked through the door, I knew somehow we could make this ours. So we have! I chattered non-stop the rest of the evening about ways *I just knew* this house could be turned into a home, regardless of the gruesome greeting we'd just received.

With a lot of help from friends and good old-fashioned elbow grease, the endeavor began. The challenge we faced included stained linoleum floors, bathrooms that leaked, and a deck so rotted that one day while I was pacing and talking on the phone, I fell through . . . right up to my waist!

As many as five multiple layers of former floor coverings and/or wallpaper had to be removed in many of the rooms! Every room was dark with depressingly somber paint or covered with cracked mirror squares (removal left half of us wounded!).

After an enormous amount of work the home began to come alive! Yours can, too! Looking through the eyes of potential made our creative process possible. My ever-optimistic outlook helped us envision a place that eventually stopped requiring daily repair. Increasingly, laughter and family spirit replaced the long hours of labor. Love transformed our house into a home. Creating a home of comfort is an attitude that opens us up to endless possibilities.

Yes, I know our furnishings, carpets, and walls will someday fade. The kitchen will cease feeding hungry souls. Music and laughter will no longer fill our rooms. But, precious memories of family and fellowship will live on forever in our hearts. That's the primary reason I want to inspire you and give you hope for your own home!

Let's go on a home redecorating adventure. Let the spirit of comfort begin in your own life . . . first in your own heart and attitudes. It will spill over onto everyone else in your home. You don't need to be torn down, bulldozed away, and rebuilt from the ground up. A comforting home is not so much *finding* the right house as *being the right person inside that house.* Most women I know would like to improve their homes, but are concerned with the things they *do*. The role of a soothing, softening woman is something you *are*. That gets us down to basic interior decorating.

Blueprints for Blessedness

When I mentioned that in a seminar recently, one woman winced and said, "If comfort starts on the inside, I've got a *lot* of interior decorating to do. Looks like I'll be busy awhile." She was right. Redecorating our attitude does take work, but the results are well worth it! If I'm ever going to create comfort in my home I must confront my own weaknesses and acknowledge vulnerable places in my own heart.

Our houses are the outward expression of our true home — that "real you" which is inside of each person. Thus, you can never put heart and soul into a house if it is not first inside you. That's what makes *your* house uniquely yours since our houses take on each owner's personality. If anger, bitterness, and strife are the condition of your heart, it makes sense that your household will take on those qualities.

If a real estate agent wanted to do a write-up on your house, what would its description say? Far beyond the physical description of your home, how would you describe the emotional environment, ambiance, and spiritual temperature? If you and I want to creatively adorn our homes, let's begin with the entrance. Upon entering, others will be inspired to spend time in your home as they are welcomed with a pleasing reception.

You have the power to lift your family's spirits or bring them down to rock bottom. I can guarantee that if you make your family's entrances a welcoming experience, they will be eager to head home often! Knowing they will enter into a shelter from the storms of life brings great comfort. We all need to take sanctuary behind doors where caring arms await to hug and hold.

A friend of mine shared an epitaph she had seen while walking through a park and adjoining cemetery.

The inscription read: SHE WAS THE SUNSHINE OF OUR HOME. Donna said the rest of her walk she kept thinking, *That's probably the last thing they'd put on my tombstone*. She determined that afternoon to be pleasant even if her house was in chaos when she returned!

You can become the sunshine in your home, but first you must learn where the clouds are. The first four minutes after arrival into the home are critical in setting the tone for the rest of the evening. If you are cheery and comforting tonight, chances are your husband and children will be. If you are gripey and growly, they probably will be too, since they take their cues from you.

Homecoming Hugs

At our house, coming home is something to celebrate! We place a high premium on respect for one another so we welcome each other home with enthusiasm. When we hear that garage door opening, it is our signal to welcome one another home eagerly. It communicates, "You were missed! I'm so glad you're home!"

I make every effort to hug each family member as they walk through our door. No, it may not always be convenient to stop what I'm doing, but I do anyway. Tender touches are ways to communicate my expressions of love. Try it — for some it will be awkward at first. It will come easier to you the more you do it. Your family will love it. What a shame that many children (adults, too) will pillow their head tonight without one hug or satisfying touch from a loved one all day long.

Everyone you live with will live a happier, healthier life from experiencing frequent touches. Scientific results indicate many emotional and health benefits from at least 8 to 12 touches a day. Fluffy animals are brought in for hospital and nursing home residents to caress and hug. It makes their day! "Hugs are the best form of emotional and physical therapy," reports Jo Lindberg, founder of the Hugs for Health Foundation.

Touch comforts. Touching gives a sense of safety and security, no matter what our age. Infants thrive when held by humans who care for them. A gentle, soothing touch upon returning home, at bedtime, and for "no reason at all" wraps us in a warm security blanket of comfort. It reassures of love, acceptance, and that *"everything's gonna be alright"* feeling.

Sometimes I may choose to pout and withdraw with a "poor me" pity party for myself. Giving in to my gripey attitude (and starting the day by slinging cereal bowls across the table) only multiplies the problem. It does not take long and we have more than one Oscar the Grouch at the breakfast table!

Things seem to start off much better when I determine to set a positive attitude first thing in the morning. In the mornings when I awake, before I crawl out of bed, I thank the God for another day and for what it will bring. Maybe I'm to clean house that day, or travel, or work in my office or meet a friend for coffee. The day's schedule is not the issue . . . my heart attitude is. "This is the day the Lord has made; let us rejoice and be glad in it" (Ps. 118:24). I have a choice to rejoice! And so do you.

Comfort Is Contagious

What is your attitude toward day-to-day life? Do you know that your personal happiness depends on the attitude you will have? It does. It's deeper than the "full cup, empty cup" outlook. It is essential that we see ourselves in light of God's true Word . . . then be open to change when change is needed.

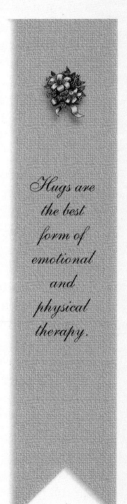

Hugs are the best form of emotional and physical therapy.

"But, nobody's perfect."

"That's just the way I am."

"I was born this way."

"If you only knew what I've been through."

"It's not my fault."

Excuses come so easily. Maybe you return home exhausted. Maybe your husband opens the front door upset and wants to pick a fight. Out of your own resources of love and by an act of your will, you can *choose* to be a blessing rather than a burden!

I know. I've had to myself. I had to just last night.

Mile-long Rooftops

During Bible days, apartment-type homes were built in and on top of the city walls. To protect the home from sun and rain, part of the roof extended beyond the walls. The word describing the overhang is "forbear," which means an "outroof." The same word is used in the command to forbear one another in love (see Eph. 4:2–3). God is telling us to outroof one another *in love.*

I had to *choose* to be a blessing of comfort in our home by "outroofing" (protecting) Rob from his fatigue after he returned home last night exhausted. He did not know how to get off the merry-go-round he had been on all week after a hectic holiday calendar of parties, appointments, and meetings. I lovingly chose to withdraw from last night's events when I realized the stress within Rob.

Sure, I wanted to go to the event . . . I was not "peopled out" since I'd been in my office alone most of the workday. But, it was just another way of saying, "I don't always have to have my way.

You are important." *Choose* to go the extra mile. It really pays off! Being comforted after his stressful day, Rob then renewed and filled our home with kindness and laughter as we chatted through the evening. I believe my determination to be a blessing, not a burden, was a good choice.

Learn to Laugh

One of the most soothing sounds you can hear upon entering your own home is laughter coming from those you love. What a lift to any heavy heart who steps inside! As we learn to bring humor into our lives, we are relaxed and put at ease.

One of the most soothing sounds you can hear upon entering your own home is laughter coming from those you love.

Laughing at yourself is great therapy for any tense situation. Our Mindy recently offered to prepare a special chicken dinner for Rob and me. I got home later than usual from an appointment to hear wails of hysteria from the kitchen. Watching to see my reaction to a huge mess upon my arrival, Mindy proceeded to describe the steps of her culinary efforts . . . and how the kitchen arrived in its present state of shambles.

Mindy's description of her clumsiness while pouring from a slippery pitcher, egg shells that wouldn't crack, and how her right hand had gotten lodged between the oven rack and cake pan were hilarious. We survived the ordeal by pitching in together for the cleanup. The more questions I asked about "How did this get *here?*" the harder we laughed.

Rob returned a half an hour later to find us both slumped into chairs, laughing to the point of tears. He said he could hear the laughter all the way from the driveway and couldn't wait to get inside! I got to hear the scenario all over again! Then, we all pitched in to be a part of the hazardous waste cleanup crew!

Laughter Comforts

The more you look for humor in life, the more you find it. Some days are so devastating you have to look pretty hard. Solomon knew what he was talking about when he said, "A cheerful heart is good medicine" (Prov. 17:22). Rob received a tonic that day when he arrived home.

Doctors agree that everyone needs to laugh more. In several Mayo Clinic Health Letters experts have reported that laughter is a wonderful antidote in curing depressing health and emotional problems. Learn to chuckle at situations that are ridiculous — it helps put your problems into perspective. And it sure is fun to return home to!

Barbara Johnson, author and humorist, says to remember:

> Laughter is like changing a baby's diaper: It doesn't permanently solve any problems, but it makes things more acceptable for a while.

Let the Light Shine Through

Smiles are a delight to come home to! Acquire the habit of smiling. Few people realize the value and power a smile can give to others! When you give a smile, you transfer attention from yourself to others. It communicates, "I'm here for you," not "What can you do for me?" Thus, your own health, joy, and self-esteem is strengthened.

Women who radiate true, timeless beauty know that secret! A smile is the outward evidence of inward joy and praise which brings glory to God. I have traveled to countries where language posed a barrier, but have never had trouble communicating if I wore a smile! Somehow, it communicates worth and encouragement in a very practical sense.

Regardless of how you feel on the inside (feelings are so fickle), learn that a smile is so important in having an abiding joy. Jesus calls it, "the abundant life." He himself designed the perfect house plans when He said, "If you remain in me and my words remain in you, ask whatever you wish, and it will be given you. . . . Ask and you will receive, and your joy will be complete" (John 15:7–16:24).

The condition for such joy is allowing Jesus to sit at the control center of your home. To relinquish those controls, you and I must depend on His sure Word of truth, no matter what comes. That's how I'll know I'm building according to His plan. It sure takes the pressure off of me. When I do take the controls back, I'm sorry I have. For I have "tasted" the abundant life and that's the kind of home I want. As King David expressed it long ago, "You have made known to me the path of life; you will fill me with joy in your presence" (Ps. 16:11).

As a light in the window beckons to those on the outside, "Someone's home, we invite you in," so a smile lights up your face giving those on the outside a message, "Love lives here. I'm here for you, I invite you into my heart." It's what I like to call a "yes" face instead of a "no" face. Approachable. Hopeful. It reaches out and touches others!

The more you look for humor in life, the more you find it.

Where Seldom Is Heard
a Discouraging Word

You may have seen the cartoon a few years ago, of a man sitting at the breakfast table reading his paper. His wife is sure he's not listening, but asks, "Are you listening to me?"

"Of course, dear," he replies without looking up.

Frustrated, she shouts, "The state inspector was here. He has condemned our house because it's being eaten by giant termites."

"Yes, dear," he replies.

Exasperated by this time, she slams down her coffee cup and stalks out of the room.

Women! Who can understand them? hubby thinks to himself, shaking his head.

Not only do some families need to smile a bit more, they need also to communicate a lot more as well. When the lines of communication are open with some "give and take" on *both* sides, there is hope for strong relationships between family members. How do you keep these lines open? May I offer a few suggestions:

WARNING! DO NOT READ THIS BOOK —

Unless, of course, you want to learn, as I am learning, some vital issues about words and speech. James tells us that the tongue is like a bit in a horse's mouth; if we control the bit, we can control the whole horse. Since I am one who tends to speak before I think, I'm trying to learn to follow the general rule from the Bible: "Whatsoever things are true . . . honest . . . just . . . pure . . . lovely . . . of good report . . . think on these things" (Phil 4:8;KJV).

This admonition sounds slightly "Pollyanna," but it miraculously brings joy to my heart. If I deliberately think "on the good" I begin to feel more kindly toward Rob and other people, too. Then, I am not so likely to tear them down.

Negative cut-downs are huge communication barriers. No one likes to carry on a conversation with someone who is negative, cutting, and discouraging. In fact, we avoid people like that. Throughout our first year of marriage, I did not know that a man cannot communicate with a negative, nagging wife. *I* was making our communication break down.

When I discovered the biblical ethic of communicating in affirming, positive ways, Rob began to talk again. His and my needs were restored and esteem confirmed in both of us. Encouraging words are meaningful gifts that can say to a needy heart, "I love you!"

I love Paul's reminder to the Thessalonians when he said, "For you know that we dealt with each of you as a father deals with his own children" (1 Thess. 2:11). A loving father gently urges his children. He encourages. He is just and uplifting. His words build up; they do not tear down.

Even as I was writing those words, the doorbell rang, and I received a note from the hands of the small daughter of a neighbor friend. The note contained some dear words of encouragement that just made my day. After doing piles of laundry, cleaning the garage, and running errands, the encouragement came when it counted!

Ask and you will receive, and your joy will be complete.

(John 16:24)

How vital are comforting, encouraging words! I recently had the privilege of spending a day with a well-known author. As I observed her life, I realized that she had developed and honed the gift of encouragement like no one I had ever seen. All day long I heard her encourage, thank, and ask insightful questions of those around her. Praise flowed naturally out of her mouth. Others wanted to be near her. She wasn't "putting on," she had literally made it a point to develop a good habit of saying encouraging words.

Proverbs tells us that the mouth of the righteous is a "fountain of life" (Prov. 10:11). I came away refreshed from being with that dear woman. Not because she's famous or an author, but, her speech filled so many thirsting hearts that day . . . mine included.

Stop! Look! Listen!

We women are often great at being preoccupied while family members are trying to talk with us. Filing our nails, talking on the phone, or thumbing through a magazine shows others disrespect and disinterest. However egotistical it may seem, each of us is delighted when another person really cares about what we are saying by *stopping* what they are doing . . . *looking* at us in the eye . . . and really *listening!*

You can put others at ease to converse — yes, even your teenagers — by finding questions designed to "draw out" the other person. By taking time out to stop what you are doing, you are creating an immediate rapport with those in your home. That's how we learn about each other . . . to really know and love each other.

Many suburban homes are silent except for the sounds of the CD player blaring, a high-speed modem punching away to download a memo, and the racket of three phone lines so tied up that Dad can't get on the web to check his e-mail. Families are spending more time communicating with electronics than with each other.

One family related to me, "Each time we come home, we each go directly to the computer, phone answering machine, or stereo. Buttons and knobs are being pushed in every room of the house. A whole evening can go by without any interaction with whoever else is in the house." Beep, beep, ring, ring, da, da, da. . . . How sad, but probably true in far too many homes.

The hum of a spiritless technological security blanket does not comfort like the soft, articulate utterance of a hug, compliment, or encouraging word.

Open House, Open Heart

The moment folks step up to your door, they are getting a glimpse of what is inside. We want our home to have an atmosphere that draws others to us . . . to open up ourselves rather than to shut others out. There are many little touches that can demonstrate that a loving attitude awaits inside, making a home's exterior entryway inviting.

I enjoy changing welcome mats and door wreaths for each season. They lend a gracious greeting to your family and guests. We (and most guests) enter through our back door so I replace them often due to the wear and tear from weather and deck travel. When selecting a welcome mat, choose one that suits your style and the message you would like conveyed to visitors.

The mouth of the righteous is a fountain of life.

(Prov. 10:11)

While clean and orderly entrances are important, it is even more important that each guest to our home senses a spirit of comfort and hope. We often have people in crisis or pain stop by for counsel. A friendly entrance puts others at ease before ever opening the door. A visual invitation of "welcome" takes very little effort, but can make a big difference.

Take time to stand outside and take a look at your front door. Walk up to it. See and feel what guests see and feel. Maybe it's time to give it a lovely new color that stands out or new brass hardware that glows with greeting!

Most of all, you yourself can become a door of *hope* to all who enter your life. Throughout Scripture, God is referred to as our spiritual safety, security, and source of comfort. We are to run to Him for rest from the storms and stresses of life. He totally accepts you. He loves you with an everlasting love. He is your refuge. He is constant and reliable . . . always there. With Him we will never know the meaning of the term "homeless" because He promises, "Never will I leave you nor forsake you" (Heb. 13:5).

Too often we believe the lie, "This is hopeless." Maybe you are really hurting and suffering today or bearing deep pains from the past . . . and the last thing on your mind is giving your front door a make-over. In fact, like many women I've met, your real fantasy is to throw in the towel and put a FOR SALE sign out in front of your house. My heart goes out to you today.

I want you to know that there *is* hope. To the extent that you will throw open wide the door of hope and walk in, you will find healing and comfort. God will transform your "Valley of Achor" (trouble) into a door of hope! (see Hos. 2:15). What a glorious promise! In the same way our hearts turn toward home for a physical refuge, we can turn to Him for comfort . . . and then begin to redecorate from the ground up!

Believe me, I know.

PERSONAL OR GROUP STUDY GUIDE • WEEK 1

1. Consider and discuss the ways that your home is a true expression of the inward "real you."

2. Think back to how your childhood home through the teen years impacts your current:
- self-worth/or lack of
- attempts to win/fight/please/argue
- responses in your present home to others
- ability or desire to be all that God intended you to be

3. In what ways could your home better express the spirit of hospitality that makes guests and family alike feel instantly welcome? (See 2 Pet. 1:12; Col. 1:10; 2 John 1:4.) Cite some practical personal examples.

4. List some qualities you would like to have inscribed on your tombstone as an epitaph. What choices will you have to make in order to possess those qualities? (Hint: read Phil. 4:8.)

5. What "praise phrase" (encouragement from family, friends, or employer) makes you do your very best job? How can you put "praise phrases" into your own words to encourage others?

6. List the ways you intend this week to redecorate your heart by having a deep and meaningful relationship with Jesus Christ.

7. Describe what you imagine your home being like in order to impact generations to come for Christ.

PARAGRAPH PRAYER
Finish writing out this paragraph prayer of thanksgiving to God for your present home: Lord help me to find contentment and overwhelm me with gratefulness in_____
_____
_____
_____

Lovingly,
Your Daughter

Dirty Windows in My Pain

One chilly fall day, I remember sitting in the living room of our Walton-style farmhouse. This was almost 20 years ago. I was not quite 30 years old, but felt 90. Looking out at the autumn wonderland sent a bittersweet ache to my heart. The world outside was so lovely, but I didn't know where or how I fit in to the world inside of me.

Sitting for hours on that sofa, I asked myself for perhaps the first time, "Who am I? Why am I here? Where am I really going?" I dared not know who the real me really was. I longed to know but was afraid of finding out. I had become a slave to what the "they" in my world would think. So used to playing the role according to what others wanted for me, *I* didn't even enjoy being around me — how could I expect my friends and family to?

So I just sat in my living room. And sat. When Rob would come home at noon I would be in the same robe, in the same chair, watching the same TV channel. It was just too much effort to get up, walk across the room and change it. (This was back in the year B.R. — Before Remote.)

I'd sit and stare out the windows. Windows, that in previous fall seasons I would have enjoyed cleaning to a bright shine. Not that fall. Like the clouded spirit inside of me, the windows of our home became more and more difficult to see clearly through. I didn't know if they would ever come clean. As the weeks passed, I didn't even care.

Existing, Not Living

Have you, too, had a difficult time putting comfort in your home because you have not met the first prerequisite: a healthy attitude and acceptance of yourself? Comfort in your own heart is necessary before there can be a comforting attitude toward others. Like I was for so long, maybe you have been unable to be positive, honest, and comfortable being the *real* you. Unable to develop my own personality and talents, frustration mounted. I stooped to be a copy of someone else rather than accept that God made me an original. My thinking had become distorted. I blamed everyone else for my pain and problems. For a long time I wallowed in the mire of self-pity, thinking I was destined to be miserable. Life was passing me by. I was existing, but not really living.

Conscious efforts by well-meaning friends and family to "fix Sharon" were to no avail. Everyone who knew me commented on how poorly I looked and asked if I was feeling all right. I'd be a wealthy woman today if I had a dime for every time I was asked that year, "Are you okay?" Admittedly, I was getting scared myself. I knew the reflection in the mirror wasn't the person I was used to seeing. I forced myself through the daylight hours, grateful when nightfall came. At least there was one escape.

After a while, sleep ceased to be the answer. I could not sleep for more than a few hours nightly and stayed up for alarming hours at a time. Decisions became impossible to make. When I did make a choice as to what to wear for the day, I would wear that outfit the whole week — making a decision to change was more than I could get through. In Rob's sincere efforts to be an encouragement, he came home at noon one day to whisk me away for lunch. Reluctantly, I went along. The look on his face that I felt responsible for was too painful not to go.

Comfort in your own heart is necessary before there can be a comforting attitude toward others.

That lunch changed the course of our next year. Staring at the menu, big ol' tears began to roll down my cheeks. I couldn't decide. Rob came to my rescue by telling the waitress I did not feel well. Choosing the first thing my eyes could focus upon, I announced I'd have the chili. Bless her heart. When the waitress returned with the news that they were all out of chili, I fell apart. Now I knew I'd have to make another choice. And I knew I couldn't.

Rob knew he had to get me home. The little waitress followed us all the way to the door, apologizing all over herself for upsetting me so.

On the way home Rob held me tenderly, but talked to me firmly. He told me we were going to go for help. We didn't know exactly where to go, but we *were* going. I had come to the end of my strength and wanted help for myself as badly as he wanted it for me. Our search began the very next day. I found myself pouring out my "symptoms" to a long-time friend of ours who was a medical doctor as well as a psychologist.

I assumed he would take x-rays, run test after test on all my body parts that were hurting, write a prescription or two, and we'd be on our way. It didn't happen that way. A short exam and blood test later, this wise doctor said aloud what Rob and I had been afraid to. "Sharon is not sick, she's depressed. Clinically depressed. She needs help — more than I can give her as an out-patient." It was difficult to hear the prognosis, but with it came a remarkable sense of hope. Hope that I might finally get help!

I had not planned to spend the next weeks in a psychiatric hospital, but in that safe place I began to heal. Unresolved anger and resentment from my painful past was causing conflict in my present relationships. My years of anger turned inward resulted in deep depression. Like looking through dirty window panes, my *problems* caused everything to look distorted. But, cleaning up the dirt inside of me began a whole new perspective. Then and only then, outside began to look brighter!

How Did I Get the Capacity to Comfort?

Just when I felt I was losing my mind, ultimately, God intervened and brought help. He has sent the Holy Spirit to be our Comforter (John 14:26). That's how I received peace and began to experience His soothing comfort.

Using dear family and friends as channels of His love, God began to comfort my sorrowful soul. Their kind practical deeds and quiet presence to listen brought hope. Did they quote Bible verses? Or did they try to analyze and explain away what was happening? No. I was in no state of mind for pious platitudes or haughty explanations.

Much to my surprise, I was assured by their loving care, that God's comfort could finally bring peace to my heart. God has since used our home to be a channel of His comfort to many sorrowing and hurting people. God "comforts us in all our troubles, so that we can comfort those in any trouble" (2 Cor. 1:4).

God comforts us to make us comforters, not to make us comfortable.

The comfort God has given us
He wants us now to share
With others who are suffering
And caught in life's despair.[1]

God comforts us to make us comforters, not to make us comfortable. Without a basic willingness and ability to care for, love, and nurture yourself, it is very difficult to achieve a deep or lasting ability to comfort others. Taking good care of yourself is the foundation on which the pathway to comforting others rests. It is not something that develops overnight or as a result of any single insight decision. But for most of us, it is a modification in our behavior. We *build gradually* through a willingness to work on a number of areas in our life.

The Best Vitamins for Your Soul

Good emotional health is a product of meeting the nutritional needs of your soul. If you wish others who live in your home to be loving, caring, and comforting people — first *you must B-ONE!* Acknowledging and meeting your own basic human needs is a way you can learn to care for yourself.

It was not until the last few decades that physiological needs were identified as essential to life. While necessary for survival, meeting these needs is also essential to your emotional well-being and a satisfying life.

Recognize what your own needs are. How many of the following do you feel are being met sufficiently in your own life?

1. Physical safety and security
2. Financial security
3. Friendships
4. Respect
5. Validation
6. Sense of belonging
7. Nurturing from others
8. Physical touching and being touched
9. Loyalty and trust
10. Sexual expression and fulfillment in marriage
11. A sense of progress of goals
12. Creativity
13. Spiritual awareness — personal relationship with your Creator-God
14. Unconditional love
15. Fun and play

Many of these needs can greatly be fulfilled right in your own home. How many of these listed needs are actually being met at this time? In what areas do you come up short or feel are mostly unmet? Learn to (1) recognize and (2) meet your basic needs as a human being. Then, and only then, you are able to care for and nurture others!

Self-nurturing Activities

By performing at least one or two items from this list or one of your own daily, you will grow in the important skill of becoming a good nurturer of yourself. You have nothing to gain except an increased esteem and positive feelings. In our world we are taught to love God and be kind to our neighbors, but somehow we have a problem with knowing how to love ourselves.

I have found that many women give and give so much to others, there is no time left for themselves. As a young wife and mother, I found I had little energy or budget left to do special things for myself. It really took its toll and I began to burn out. As I began to take a more wholesome approach to this area of caring for myself, I found more satisfaction in every area. As I speak in front of various groups, I meet many women who are discouraged and defeated from juggling their many roles in life. When they learn to care for themselves because they are important in God's eyes, they are much more apt to avoid burnout and defeat. We must plan time in each of our days *to care for ourselves.* Some comforting, fun ideas to get you started include:

Learn to recognize and meet your basic needs as a human being.

- Take a warm bath
- Make #1 a bubble bath
- Buy that bundle of flowers you usually pass up
- Go to a zoo
- Have a manicure or pedicure
- Get up early and watch the sunrise outside
- Buy yourself something on your lunch hour (you can afford!)
- Swing in the park (one of my personal favorites)
- Work on a favorite puzzle
- Go to a hot tub or Jacuzzi
- Take a brisk walk listening to an affirmation tape
- Walk the beach
- Begin planning this summer's vacation
- Browse in a card, garden, gift, or book shop
- Write an encouraging card to a friend
- Rent a good film or feel-good movie
- Dawdle — take more time than you need to accomplish whatever chore you're doing
- Visit a museum or city landmark
- Listen to a positive, motivational tape
- Write in your journal
- Apply fragrant lotion all over your body
- Exercise
- Sit and hold your puppy
- Go to bed early
- Fix a special dinner, eat by candlelight
- Sleep out under the stars
- Take a scenic drive around a lake
- Go to a fine restaurant or tea room — just with yourself
- Grill out — watch the sun set

Others contribute to but cannot meet your deep needs of adequacy and confidence. Only God truly can. He has put within each of us a void that only He can fill. He is

always there, patiently waiting for us to turn to — and run to — Him. When you do, joyous acceptance, respect, and validation of being *you* re-affirms and strengthens a positive attitude and feelings about yourself. God loves you, He accepts you, He sees you! Psalms 147 is an intimate love letter from your Heavenly Father confirming that!

Customized Comfort

Honoring your own needs contributes greatly to personal wellness. Daily focusing on taking care of your needs will have a direct impact on the level of comfort in your home. Four areas which involve different levels of your whole being include:

> BODY: Physical body and well-being
> FEELINGS: Your emotional self-expression
> MIND: Positive affirmations
> SOUL: Personal relationship with the Savior

Just like a fine piece of machinery, each part must run properly for us to perform as God intended. It's likened to a four-legged stool. If one leg is weak or too short, no one better try sitting on it!

Most women I know want to be capable, confident, effective, and strong. Naturally, the more you care for yourself, the more confident you will be! We sabotage comfort right in our own homes when we do not practice personal wellness. Daily. It's that simple! No matter how good your intentions may be, no woman can handle the stress of managing a home when she has not given herself vital opportunity for essential refueling.

Be creative in this area, but don't forget the obvious. I began a practice of sound mind and body habits quite out of necessity. My own negative self-talk, destructive health and sleep patterns, along with a "victim" ("poor me") attitude had begun to render me hopeless and powerless. Days of depression led to weeks, and I was gradually "stuck" — unable to move out of the doubt, fear, and despair.

Every woman I have ever known has dealt with depression to some extent. Many battle with it monthly like clockwork. Overcoming the problem is never a singular task. I had to learn to rely on family and a very godly friend-counselor whom I respected. Through very small steps at first, we developed a plan of action to find my way out of the numbed-out emotional state.

I then had a "map" to follow. Not groping in darkness any longer, I began to see rays of light. Fear finally diminished. Hope returned! To this day, I still refer to the "map" when I get stuck on obstacles along life's way.

Too Pooped to Ponder?

By far, the foundational starting point on that map to achieving peace is *setting an actual appointment with God every day.* I have found that setting a specific appointment time (the night before) to meet with God really helps me stay committed. If one of us is not there, guess who is the "no show"? I don't dare stand up the Lord! I need to settle my heart with God before the day begins with its constant interruptions, phone calls, and unexpected surprises. He, too, longs to fellowship with me!

Start small so you won't get overwhelmed and discouraged. Choose a specific amount of time that will be your set appointment time. This used to sound unappealing to me, but I found that I need the structure — it increases the probability of my actually keeping my appointment.

We could all give up 15 minutes a day of sleep or another activity in order to slip away (you'll find yourself slipping in more time many days!). A sense of direction, a plan, can make the difference between a home of comfort and just surviving the day! To generate peace in my own heart that will eventually carry over into relationships, I must first meet with the Prince of Peace. "My peace I give to you," He promises (John 14:27).

Keeping your appointment daily with your Heavenly Father will have a direct impact on your home's comfort level, as well as contribute substantially to your own well-being. Spend that time reading His love letter to you, His Word. Come away nurtured, cherished, ready to face the day because you have laid it out before the Lord. You're cultivating a relationship with the Lord of the universe. That is truly astounding.

Meet Him with an attitude of anticipation. Imagine Him sitting across the table or with you on your sofa. He is a personal God. He is not some unfamiliar, distant stranger that we awkwardly approach in fear and trembling. As you spend time with Him and His words spend time in you, you will enjoy the intimacy of the closest of relationships.

God has put within each of us a void that only He can fill.

Practice Makes Perfect

It's like any discipline. In order to follow through with a personal commitment, we must structure in a time block. I actually put my "morning watch," as Andrew Murray called his time with God, right in my day-timer. Otherwise, my time with God dwindles down to no time with God at all.

Build in variety, set times, regular evaluation, goals, and the proper tools: non-distracting setting . . . Bible . . . journal . . . autobiographies of great men and women of the faith. You are cultivating a relationship with the Lord of the universe. Holding a conversation with Him, sharing your hopes, dreams, and affections, listening to His affections for you . . . that's a daily appointment you can't miss!

I find that the combination of *daily prayer and Bible reading* has made it much more natural for me to make running to God my first response when in the midst of uncontrollable circumstances. I'm reminded that nothing — not death nor life, nor principalities, nor languid prayer and half-hearted Bible study — will be able to separate me from God's constant and abiding love.

"I will not forget you! See, I have engraved you on the palms of my hands" (Is. 49:15–16).

When I stand to sing a solo, I jot the first few words of the song on my hand just to get me going. God has engraved us on his loving palms!

God's Word is always timely and comforting! My Bible is splashed with underlined verse and ink marks next to verses of hope during times I need a lift. That is why it is so important to develop one's own regular Bible-reading plan. Always timely and comforting, we can run to Him — for His promises are there to catch us during any fall.

Your Dream Home

What a way to bring comfort to your home . . . from the inside out! It is impossible to over-emphasize the immense need humans have for security. Comfort brings that reassurance; you feel safe and protected from the storms of life. The beautiful thing is that the more secure we feel in our home life, the more confidence we have to live life beyond the walls of our home. The door to comfort is really there waiting for any of us to open and go through.

What does it take to find comfort at your own address? Several things. Rare, beautiful qualities in a woman. Like time. Hugs. Listening. Care. Unselfishness. Encouragement. Laughter. And perhaps, most of all, letting yourself rest securely and comfortably in the hands of God.

> A house is made of
> walls and beams,
> A home is built with
> love and dreams.

When Your Home Is Falling Apart

Whatever else might be said about home, it is the number one place where I long to be when I have been on the road traveling very long. I've seen and been to some awesome places and am very blessed to have met some wonderful friends away from my home. The plain and simple truth remains as accurate today as the day Dorothy said it in *The Wizard of Oz:* "There's no place like home!"

When I've been gone "flying the friendly skies" for very long, my own bed and warm fireplace feels pretty good. Be it ever so humble, there's just no place like it! Recently, I returned after a week-long exhausting ministry trip to find flowers blooming everywhere that hadn't even budded when I left. What a welcome! Grabbing my camera, I ran out to the front of the house and snapped a picture. I felt like Jimmy Stewart as he raced throughout his house after the realization of what home truly meant to him. "I love you, you old house!" he cried . . . broken banister railing and all!

Chaos. Yes. I returned to my home's comforts, but also to its concerns. So much for the photo opportunity. The very

I have engraved you on the palms of my hands.

(Isa. 49:16)

next day, real life rushed in. I wanted to cry. I began to understand what I read the other day on a bumper sticker. It read: "Life is like ice cream. Just when you think you have it licked, it drops all over you."

My morning started out like the recitation of "You know you're going to have a bad day when. . . ." First, I put both contacts in ONE eye. Then hurriedly, I began to make the first of eight calls I needed to return, each one to hurting people that took longer than usual to counsel. On to the long distance calls — only to discover our long distance service was down temporarily. Groan. All morning I kept looking for just a little encouragement, some small joy.

But, that day it seemed as if finding joy was not going to be an easy thing to do. I was already way behind by noon, but headed out to run errands anyway.

The cleaners had lost Rob's favorite shirt. I managed grocery shopping (yes, my cart had those wheels on it that go in every direction). Having misplaced my grocery list, this stop took twice as long trying to shop by memory. (I just knew I'd brought that sticky note with me.) The kind gentlemen behind me in the line found it for me . . . right on the seat of my pants! To top it off, going through the fast food drive-up lane for my chicken salad, the wooden railing reached out and grabbed the entire length of the car. Rob's car. Rob's brand-new, two-week-old car!

Frazzled, Frustrated, and Frantic

With tears having ruined my mascara and my best-laid plans scrapped, I returned home wondering how the day could ever be salvaged. Life and its upsets seemed to be gaining momentum. By the end of that day, everything I'd tried to accomplish was in chaos and I was frazzled, frustrated, and frantic!

What a blessing when my eye caught sight of a visible reminder of how special I am to God. It was the shiny red plate in my china hutch on which is engraved: "You are special today!" I'm sure you have heard of these plates and may

even have one yourself. They are designed after a custom among early American families. When someone in our home deserves special praise or attention, our custom is to serve their meal on the special plate.

Oh, how I needed this reminder right then! Its message caused me to remember that today and *every day* I am special to God. It just seemed to wrap me in the comfort of God's love. Even if it isn't my birthday, or Mother's Day, or when I've accomplished something outstanding, God's love is still the same *every day*. With tears welling up in my eyes I paused to drink in the red plate's message.

Not much else seemed to go right in our home that entire week. I made a point to pause often in front of our red plate to let God's comfort blanket wrap around me again and again. I truly believe God cares for us and uses even the smallest of things to reveal His love.

I know there are a lot of bigger problems in the world, but mine had piled up so high that I could not see past them. I want to remind you of how special you are today — to me and to God — you ARE a Somebody! How I wish I could reach out to everyone hurting right now and serve each one of you a lovely meal on your very own shiny red plate. As I've had to at the close of many a growly day, you can get a fresh start. Accept what you cannot change, and with God's help, put the past behind you. You can, if you will:

TRACE IT! — Trace your problem to the root of your pain. You might be shocked to find out that what you are allowing to dominate your life is not the real problem at all. Until I got a grasp on the pain of insecurities from abandonment in my young years, I could not trust others,

God, or my husband. I assumed they would not be there for me someday but would leave me abandoned. When I traced fears that had been embedded for so long, I could then escape from them. And, more importantly, move on! Past pain does not have to have a grasp on every aspect of your life.

FACE IT! — Take positive action steps to amend, forgive, then remove whatever it is that paralyzes you with heartache and fear. It is much easier to submit to emotional surgery for removal of the turmoil, than to let the harmful disease fester forever, infect, and eventually inflame every area of your life.

ERASE IT! Surrender your "it" to the Lord and He will wipe the slate clean with His special eraser called FORGIVENESS. What is "it" that holds you captive? You cannot conquer pain, injury, suffering, and anxiety in your own strength. Only God can truly set us free . . . remarkably free from even the memory of your pain! There isn't any situation so bad that it can't be forgiven. Keeping your "it" bottled up inside will only make you bitter. First, we must relinquish. Give your pain away. No more rehashing and reviewing . . . it is no more. Where once you felt pain's icy fingers, God will hold you in His everlasting arms. "I sought the Lord, [TRACE IT!] and he answered me; [FACE IT!] he delivered me [ERASE IT!] from all my fears" (Ps. 34:4)

The Best Security System You Can Install

Dear Reader, your life's predicament may be full of "unexpecteds" such as the day I just described, or there may be blows more severe than you can bear. Losses, calamitous illness, release from a job, sudden death . . . your home may be falling apart. If you are not experiencing a trial today, hold on! You will be soon! That's life! Scripture tells us that we will not escape trouble and to not think it strange when fiery trials come upon us (Ps. 34 and 2 Pet. 4). There will come a time when your faith is severely tested. Remember, life is not fair. But, God is!

A Home Built to Last

May I carefully share a biblical principle that will uphold and sustain you in a day of trouble? The bedrock, incredible truth is: *When everything or everyone else seems against you, God is for you!*

Life is like ice cream. Just when you think you have it licked, it drops all over you.

What wonderful good news! That God is FOR us, not against us (Rom. 8:31). I can think of nothing more assuring and securing. He really is a God I can trust. He's shown me time and time again by what He has done in my own home in the face of pain, doubt, and despair. I've seen God prove himself over and over.

Storms come, winds blow, and the rains descend upon all of our homes. Both houses described in Matthew 7 were rained upon, indicating that no home is exempt from storms. Life just seems to go from one extreme to another. The foolish builder hurries, putting materials together in a "hodgepodge" way. Here . . . there . . . whatever is available at the time or easiest. When the rains come, that house falls.

I can remember singing the chorus about the foolish man who "built his house upon the sand." I loved when we came to the part, "And the house on the sand went SPLAT!" We'd give a big clap and fall down out of our seats.

But . . . the wise man built his house upon the rock. Yes, his faith was under attack outside the four walls of his home. He had to constantly fight against the onslaught of the world's philosophies that stormed down upon his rooftop. The song chants, "And the house on the rock STOOD FAST!" It did not fall because its foundation was Jesus Christ, the Rock.

"Lord, You are my rock and my fortress and my deliverer; my God, my rock, in whom I take refuge" (Ps. 18:2; Deut. 32:4; Ps. 27:5).

Talk about home security — a home built on Jesus Christ will last! Even when the floods come, as they did in our home here in Des Moines in 1993. Our family experienced great loss of the entire downstairs level of our home during state-wide flooding. Many of our personal belongings, pictures, Christmas decorations, clothing, and household items were ruined. I grieved at the sight of these material possessions as they lay six days in separate piles until the insurance adjuster could get to our home.

These losses hurt deeply, especially the sentimental items that could never be replaced. But, our true home, that which is in the hearts of Rob, Sharon, Missy, and Mindy, that love withstood the flood waters. Our home had been built upon the Rock — we stood secure.

Homing Instinct

No person, event, or circumstance can thwart God's good plan for your life because He is for you. Even when everything seems to work against you. Jeremiah 29:11 promises, "For I know the plans I have for you . . . plans to give you hope and a future." You can stop nailing yourself to a cross because Jesus was nailed to one for you. You can live a guilt-free life from here on out! When we do sin, we have an advocate with God, the Father — His Son, Jesus Christ. That's why you can keep coming to God for complete forgiveness. No, you cannot change the past, but you can get full forgiveness for what happened in the past (see 1 John 1:9, 2:1). That hope is better home improvement than any restoration job you can tackle.

What are you a captive of? Name it, then turn yourself over to God, surrendering all, and He will set you free! Trust in His love and character. Joy will return! I had let Rob down. But, you see, I trust Rob profoundly. I trust in his love and his character enough to know that he wants the best for me. I know that his love goes deeper than my scratching his car. Trusting someone means you risk. You risk being let down, betrayed, or hurt.

He will wipe the slate clean with His special eraser called forgiveness.

Perhaps that's why the trust of a little child is so precious. A small child trusts that we will catch them when they jump into our arms. They just jump! In their child-like vulnerability they trust. Unfortunately, these days we have to teach them that you can't just trust anybody. "You could be hurt, cheated, even murdered," we're forced to warn.

You know what it's like to be betrayed by someone you trusted. I can still feel the hurt, disappointment, and fear I felt as a young child spending my first few years in inconsistency. My mother had contracted tuberculosis when it was rampant in the fifties, shortly after I was born. For some months doctors sent her for therapy and rest at a sanitarium in a nearby city. I knew that my mother loved me, but I couldn't trust her at the age when I felt like separation was abandonment and rejection.

I was sent from one relative or church member's house to another, since my daddy pastored a new, struggling work and could not feasibly take care of my sister and me at such young ages. No one was able to keep us very long. After all, they had their families and lives to lead. So we spent a short while at each willing person's home, then were moved on. I thought it was me. I thought no one wanted me. I must have been in the way, too much trouble.

Finally we were back together as a family. But, the consistency did not last very long, My lack of trust deepened. My mother got sick again, this time with polio. I couldn't even trust her to go on living. Mother died when I was just three. To a child, the death of a parent is the ultimate betrayal. Even though my daddy did the best he knew to help my sister and I feel secure, we had lost the security that only a mother can bring to a child. I felt abandoned.

I didn't know how to grieve. In fact, I was playing "funeral" with my dolls in shoe boxes the day after Mother was buried. It wasn't until many years later that I was guided to grieve the loss and begin the long journey of learning to trust. Placing a rose at her grave with my dear daddy standing at my side began the healing process — for which I am eternally grateful. Then and only then, was I able to begin loving and trusting the dear mother God had given us as a gift from Him.

No, my situation did not change. I chose to forgive my mother for dying. After all, it was not her choice. It happened. My attempts to discern or understand were futile. But, my choice to accept changed everything! When my trust factor was restored, I could trust God as well. After all, He is for me, not against me (see Is. 43:1–3 and Ps. 118:6).

I can trust God because of what He is and because of what He has done. He has shown me who He is and proven many, many times that He is trustworthy. To me the most incredible part is that He will never abandon me or reject me. I am loved and redeemed by God; His Word tells me so. Perhaps the greatest theology I've ever learned is in the little Sunday school chorus, "Jesus loves me this I know, for the Bible tells me so."

God really is a parent I can trust. He's shown me His trustworthiness by what He has done in my life and in the lives of so many people I know. I think of so many people — young moms, single parents, parents looking for their prodigals, men and women with life-threatening illnesses. They are an example for me of God's care in their weakness and pain. He will do the same for you! God has given you all you need to confidently trust Him. In His Word we're promised:

Jesus loves me this I know, for the Bible tells me so.

> • His presence: "I will never leave you nor forsake you" (Josh. 1:5).
> • His provision: "I was young and now I am old, yet I have never seen the righteous forsaken or their children begging bread" (Ps. 37:25).
> • His protection: "The Lord is my light and my salvation. . . . The Lord is the strength of my life; of whom shall I be afraid?" (Ps. 27:1; KJV).

Trust is the antithesis of fear. This is a God who has given me the assurance of His presence when I give Him my trust. When I look back at the way my life has unfolded, I stand astonished at the goodness and mercy He shows. He is constantly releasing streams of blessings my way! To this woman who distrusted everyone and had good reason to, He has healed that distrust by giving me a new mother, a faithful daddy, and a strong, dependable, nurturing husband whom I am able to trust without reservation.

This same trustworthy God transformed a willing but inexperienced young wife and put her in ministry with her best friend. Then, He gave her the opportunity to teach others what she has learned through a nationwide ministry of writing and speaking. My cup runneth over!

How about you? Are you having a hard time trusting . . . trusting God . . . or your husband . . . or those in your past? God is able to run this universe and He certainly is capable of taking all the pain and fears in your heart and turning them into "exceedingly abundantly more than you can ask or think" (Eph. 3:20). His goodness, even in the most painful hour, pursues you to comfort and settle you.

What to Do When Your House Is Falling Apart

I think of my friend Denise Chapman. No, her house didn't blow down or fall down, but the very foundation was shaken two years ago. She was making her weekly jaunt to Wal-Mart like so many of us American women do. Having a little extra time this day, she allowed her two year old the privilege of riding the merry-go-round in front of the store. Tenderly she placed the baby carrier with six-month-old Nathaniel resting quietly inside on the pavement beside her foot. Turning to place the quarters in the machine, she watched Jonathan smile as he anticipated the ride.

In split-second timing Denise heard the loudest noise she's ever heard coming from behind her. She caught sight of the car speeding toward and crashing into the wall of Wal-Mart, carrying with it the precious cargo of Nathaniel in his carrier. At the same time the car, whose accelerator had stuck, brushed across Jonathan's leg, severing it just above the kneecap.

I can't even begin to describe the agony of this young family's loss. Nathaniel was killed instantly. Jonathan, now two years later, plays as happily as any other little fella — when he gets tired of his prosthesis, he just removes it and props it up in the corner awhile. The trust in God's sovereignty is a dramatic witness to God's trustworthiness. He has been this home's firm rock, a sure foundation. He has proven to be their door, their way, truth, and life, their secure rock upon which to stand — even on days they feel like they are going to fall.

For I know the plans that I have for you.

(Jer. 29:11)

I wondered how they would ever learn to function in joy again. But, they have! What a privilege it has been to see God provide through the past two years. He has been with them through their pain, and now through their gains. In January of this year, God blessed them with little Hannah. Even her name is a tribute to God's reliability.

There is not a time that I enter a Wal-Mart now that my eye does not catch sight of the yellow posts that are protective barriers so that such a tragedy might never happen again. Nor is there a time that I do not pause to praise God for His constant reminders in our lives that He can be trusted. Then I pause to ask His special sweetness to be upon Denise's family that day.

Take a look at the word "sovereign." Underline the last five letters. R-E-1-G-N. Without letting God reign "supremely, above all others," as Webster's says of the meaning of the word, we are doing the reigning, not Him. We must give Him the reins, if you will, to reign!

As a result of trusting, my life is much more peaceful. He knew what was best all the time. Oh, sometimes I think I do, but God has a clearer sense of the beginning AND the end. That's why I must trust as an act of my free will. It forces me to grow. There's no place I can go that He will not be with me. There are still times my pain of living in uncertain homes my first few years of life wraps over me like a blanket of betrayal.

Do I have to run back to my Heavenly Father for my comfort?

Of course, I do. Every single day.

The master architect lovingly restores — putting more security into our home than any infrared sensor mounted to a transmitter that beams up to 100 feet away! And there are no batteries needed. Just complete childlike trust.

Personal or Group Study Guide • Week 2

1. According to 2 Cor. 1:4, God comforts us not necessarily to *be* comforted, but to _____ others in time of trouble. How has a painful experience of misery in your life become a ministry of comfort to others in need?

2. Paul said, "For we are His *workmanship* created in Christ Jesus to do good works . . ." (Eph 2:10). The word "workmanship" brings the idea of a *"work of art."* Recognizing that you are God's *masterpiece work of art*, how are you fulfilling God's purpose for your life?

3. What sound mind, body, and soul personal wellness habits are you creating in your life to refuel?
* Daily actual "appointment" with God
* Cultivating friendships
* Barring negative, destructive self-talk
* Healthy exercise and sleep habits
* Setting boundaries in career and outside-the-home commitments

4. Have storms beat upon your heart's door? Discuss how God can possibly be using *everything* for your good by first thinking back to a situation that was really bad and something good came of it, perhaps years later (Rom. 8:28).

5. God is not mad at you for failures or discouragements. In fact, He's mad *about you!* He will do whatever it takes to bring you into intimate fellowship with himself and to help you live up to your God-given purpose. Read aloud the verses Jer. 1:5 and Jer. 29:11. Is your daily schedule indicative of these desires and dreams God has for you?

PARAGRAPH PRAYER
Finish writing this paragraph prayer of genuine acceptance: Father, with joy and gratitude, I accept the transforming truth that You have "wonderfully and fearfully" made me to fulfill Your purpose even in the midst of _____
_____
_____

Lovingly,
Your Daughter

My Very Scary Hall Closet

Not so long ago as our guests stood to leave, all I remember Rob saying was, "Let me get you an umbrella. It's really pouring out!" Then he turned to me to find out exactly where the umbrellas were. I was busted. Ugh! That hall closet was really scary. I certainly did not want all my company seeing the dead, rotting . . . who knows what all was in there.

My intentions were good. I *meant* to get to cleaning closets. Sometime. Tomorrow. You know how it is. There are just certain places in our house that are the last to be tended to . . . and THAT closet was one of them. "That's okay," responded our guest, reading my thoughts (or the look of sheer panic on my face). I watched them start out the door in the pouring rain . . . vowing to clean closets tomorrow!

The very next day humiliation drove me to tackle cleaning the hall closet first. It WAS scary! Winter coats, gloves and scarves, tennis rackets, extra coffee maker — to name a few of the treasures I found. The first thing I did was take everything OUT. Then I cleaned, even painted, and placed only the useful necessities back inside. The whole hallway smelled fresh when we walked by.

One closet led to another. After inventorying each room, I cleaned closet by closet with each family member in tow. We added some super wardrobe organizers and were amazed at the space they provided. Re-organizing clothes by putting three boxes nearby worked well for us. One box was marked "to give to friends," one box marked "Salvation Army," one box marked "seasonal." We all now rotate seasonal clothing between the storage room and bedroom closets to provide better organization and more space.

If you do not have adequate storage space, purchase inexpensive standing or hanging wardrobe "closets" for easy alternating of seasons. We wrote "summer" and "winter" on the lids of storage boxes, as well, and just turn the lid around for whichever season is applicable for sweaters and other stored folded clothing.

I like what Emile Barnes has for a closet motto: "When something new comes in, something old goes out . . . too many is too many!" When we purchase or receive gifts of underwear, ties, nighties, shoes, etc. — when the new one goes in, an old one goes out! Simplify . . . simplify . . . simplify. Saves space and clutter!

When something new comes in — something old must go out!

Clutter-Free Closets

Are you using all your closet space? How about storage boxes on the top shelf, more rods and hooks for the children's rooms? Shoe trees? And if you can, buy padded hangers for dress wear and plastic ones for sports wear. Give all those wire ones back to the cleaners.

Is everything within reach, or are you having to make a lot of steps when dressing? Maybe the furniture needs rearranging for more convenience. Important note: if you live with a husband, be sure he has ample space for organization and dressing. Many times women are concerned about their needs in "their home." Consideration for your husband's needs will show him silently how important he is to you.

Maybe you want to go all out and re-paper your closet with perfumed paper, with matching paper and ribbon and border for shelves and shoe boxes. You know how far and how creative you want to go in this area. The ideas are endless. I find that when I have something decorated I tend to keep it better organized.

If you haven't worn items in your closet in a year, why haven't you? Too loose, too tight? That's another whole area you need to lay out before the Lord and discuss with your doctor. There are so many books on the subject of proper weight control. A wonderful one that friends of mine use is called "First Place." It contains terrific practical, medical, and spiritual guidance for submitting the control of your weight and healthy eating to the Lord. And I'm just as emphatic about encouraging its use for the worrier, anorexic, or bulimic woman who's too thin!

No problem is too big for God. He wants you to be a radiant picture and healthy advertisement of His care for His own.

Now step back from your closet. Is there a nearby full-length mirror? Is there a place for everything and everything in its place? Is there adequate lighting? Or are you like I was and couldn't tell the navy from the black pump? Yep, I did wear one of each to church, and yes, it was the Sunday I was to sing a solo!

Whoa! I should have cleaned my closets sooner. But, with great satisfaction, I stood back, stretched my arms and said, "Well done. No one else may know, but I know that the hidden parts of my home are clean!" What a comforting feeling. I like being clean from the inside out.

Cleaning All My Heart's Closets

I draw comfort today knowing that God will cleanse and entirely clean all the "closets" of my heart as well. No matter what junk I have stored — failures, unkindnesses of others that hurt so much, memories that won't go away, regrets, putrefying sins — I know He cares.

When I allow Jesus to open my heart's door, I can give you my word — there's no better closet cleaning! Even when I get all tied up in theological knots over the meaning of the word, Jesus *still forgives*, cleans, and washes me as white as snow.

Have you cleaned your closets of the past? I mean, really let Christ clean and move on? Paul encourages us in Philippians as he wrote of reaching forward to what lies ahead. He says to forget the past! Perhaps today many of your joy-stealers are memories that continue to haunt your mind. Why in the world do we keep bringing them up? Paul's analogy is clear. In this race called life, we are to face forward like a runner, not backward (Phil. 3:7–9).

The Power of a Flower

There's no place I can go that He will not be with me.

The day Rob returned home to find radical changes in our closets, he also found me a changed woman! "You sure are happy . . . you're like a time-release capsule ready to explode!" And explode I did . . . as I took him room by room to view my day's work on closets. In each room I received vocal bouquets of praise. It may sound silly, but Rob's words rang in my ears for the next few days.

Here I was, just performing an ordinary, menial task that met the needs of our family. I wasn't expecting recognition or glory. But this simple mundane act of service seemed to demonstrate to my husband an expression of my love. Rob filled my cup to overflowing with praise. His words spurred me on to show even more acceptance and appreciation for our home.

I hope I'm learning to do that. Ladies, taking care of and adding special comfort touches to our homes shows that we are content with what we have and where we are. Discontent with our homes and possessions often indicates a self-centered attitude which leads to malicious feelings. So often wives tend to take their homes for granted and begin losing their attitude of gratitude.

I know one such woman. She relayed her story to me at one of my women's conferences. Here was a woman who "had it all" — nice home with ocean view . . . handsome provider for a husband . . . polite children who appeared to have just stepped out of a magazine. But, this young wife looked well beyond her 35 years of age. "I had the attitude 'Who needs him?' " she told me tearfully. "But, now I realize how terrible I'd feel if he treated me the way I've treated him. Our marriage is in trouble. Do you think it's too late?"

No . . . no, I don't! Appreciation and praise motivate! That principle of human nature is as old as the hills, yet we all need to be reminded again and again.

Previously, I mentioned the cheery touch that flowers bring to a home. Even more powerful is the thankful heart which does more to keep a home healthy than any other attitude in life. I have marveled at the lack of sensitivity in some relationships. Like the couple we were with at an out-of-town meeting recently. See if you've been there, too.

Me and My Ego

When the dinner arrived at our table I watched as the wife pushed aside her plate. "Oh, ick!" With utter disdain she began her cutting speech (I could tell it had been given many times before) about who was to "blame" for this poor steak. The restaurant, cook, or the cow . . . or her husband for choosing the place? I sat squirming uncomfortably, wondering why "fixing blame" was even necessary.

The evening ended with never a word of thanks or even a hint of appreciation for being treated to such a lovely place. I'm sure he will not invite her to do so again soon!

A man has a deep need in his nature to GIVE to and provide for those he loves. He finds great joy in seeing your positive response, excitement, and thanks. With thanks and gratitude, he will give and give to the best of his ability. Without it, he stops giving and misses out on having that need of human nature fulfilled.

Until I learned this truth I failed to express appreciation for what Rob did, even if I did not like the gift. One night Rob excitedly leaped in the front door waving some tickets in his hand, yelling, "I got some! I got some! Two tickets to Saturday night's gospel concert! They've been sold out for weeks! Now we get to go!"

My expression alone was enough to put out his enthusiastic fire. I made sure he could tell I was completely unimpressed. I blurted out a comment about going anyway, but I thought he knew after all these years that I didn't like that singing group! He wilted on the spot.

We went to the concert . . . and a good time was had by all. NOT. I had committed the ultimate turnoff. Reluctant to be excited about something that meant a lot to Rob, I was unreasonable. After all, we do a lot of things that are my ideas. I'd become a taker, not a giver. So I put down my pride and asked Rob for forgiveness. I ended up having a great time at the concert . . . because I chose to! There were a lot of people there we knew and hadn't seen in a while whom I enjoyed seeing. The concert actually ministered to and encouraged my heart more than I dreamed possible.

"Giving is often misunderstood as giving up something, being deprived of, sacrificing," writes Erich Fromm in *The Art of Loving*. Instead, he describes giving as the "highest expression of potency." "In the very act of giving," he writes,

"I experience my strength, my wealth, my power. Giving is more joyous than receiving, not because it is a deprivation, but in the act of giving lies the expression of my aliveness."[2]

It was Helen Keller who said, "Life is an exciting business and most exciting when it is lived for *others.*" Keeping that thought in mind we can pray from a heart of sincerity:

> Lord, help me to live from day to day
> So that even when I kneel to pray,
> My prayer will be for *others.*
>   (Source unknown)

Giving Comforts

If we lost everything tomorrow, Rob and I would love being together and starting all over again and getting to this same point the second time around! Giving to someone you love does not make a woman subservient. Submission is not subservience. That denotes involuntary action; giving is voluntary. When I give out of love or "give in" voluntarily, I am adapting. That is not being a doormat.

The principle of submission is not my original idea; I personally don't even like the idea at times. But, I do know that when I submit as admonished in Scripture, I am giving and adapting by choice. I find that my husband is not unreasonable. In fact, frequently he changes his mind and does exactly what I wanted to do all along.

When I choose to accept Rob's plan, it's my decision. I must admit, however, that when I first learned "submission" in the Bible, I misunderstood it to mean "against my will." Many women mis-read it that way. They think their husband might become a dictator and walk all over them. That's never happened once in my marriage. In fact, the opposite.

You ask, "Isn't one-sided giving unfair? How come I have to do the submitting?" The apostle Peter had something to say about this. He said: "Wives . . . be submissive to your husbands so that, if any of them do not believe the word, they may be won over without words by the behavior of their wives" (1 Pet. 3:1). This is not an easy assignment. But, the responsibility is clearly upon the wife, not the husband.

To live a life that will challenge him to make his own decision, wives must manifest a spirit of meekness and submission. He does not see that in the world or perhaps in you before making such a conscious determination. That's why the impact is so great. This cannot be done by nagging or lecturing, but by submission. A "me Tarzan, you Jane" attitude? Nonsense! A mature, adult, loving, sharing, mutually submitting attitude is what the Bible teaches (Phil 2:3–5; 1 Pet. 3:7).

A giving woman's beauty is unfading and never more evident, according to 1 Peter 3:1–4. The description there is that she is of great worth in God's sight! Once I took the first step in an effort to adapt to Rob, to my wonderment, he became an incredibly responsible husband! Submitting is not giving for the sake of getting; that is manipulation. But, I'm continually amazed to see how my own cup overflows when I fill Rob's first!

Life is an exciting business, and most exciting when it is lived for others.

— *Helen Keller*

A Place Where Christ Lives

There is a story told of a wealthy man who purchased a famous picture of Jesus for a very high price. With its ornate frame and beautiful coloring, he sought to hang it in a prominent place in his home. Finally, out of desperation, he called an interior designer. After careful examination of the house and painting, the designer said, "You just cannot make this picture fit into your house! You must make the home fit the picture."

Just so, we must each make our lives "fit" a testimony of a healthy, stable, peaceful, loving home . . . a family centered home where there is a sense of solidarity and mutual respect . . . a home where the family does things together and has a fun time doing them.

If we have invited Christ into our lives, it goes without saying that we should invite Him into our homes. Logically then, if our life is new, shouldn't our home be also?

If Jesus came to your house
     to spend a day or two . . .
I wonder what you'd do?
Oh, I know you'd give your nicest room
     to such an honored guest.
And all the food you'd serve to Him
     would be the very best,
And you'd keep assuring Him
     you are glad to have Him there.
But, when you saw Him coming,
     would you meet Him at the door?
With arms outstretched in welcome
     to our heavenly visitor?
Or hide some magazines and put
     the Bible where they'd been?
Would you hide your worldly music
     and put a hymn book out?
Could you let Jesus walk right in,
     or would you rush about?
It might be interesting to know the things
     that you would do,
If Jesus came in person to spend some time with you.
          — Author unknown (abridged)

Retreats for Rest, Restoration, and Romance

With enough stimulation in the world today, I really need my bedroom to be an incredible relaxing place. A place to find stillness. Tranquillity. Comfort. A place where the rest of the world just seems to melt away. Sound like a dream? Dreams can come true in your own private chambers — your cozy, comfortable bedroom.

Secluded from the clamor of constant noise, I can retreat to my bedroom . . . and close the door. My physical and inner life gets nurtured in this room. Every day begins and ends here. I leave my bedroom ready to go out to face a challenging, sometimes confusing world. For that reason I have filled our bedroom with decor of harmonious colors that gently beckons me to rest and unwind perhaps more than any other room in our home.

A bedroom needs to be a place where the rest of the world just seems to melt away.

Before I set up my own housekeeping I listened to women as they guided me through their homes. In united agreement, they voiced their desire to spend decorating efforts and funds on every "seen" room in the house first. Consistently the bedroom received attention last. "After all, no one sees that room except my husband and me."

How sad! I vowed that when I married I would make sure to create a bedroom of beauty with indulgences as wonderful as the sweet dreams we would dream there. That has been my inspiration for all these many years. Even though my bedroom is the least likely room to be seen by guests, its four walls are the first thing Rob and I see each morning.

If you are undergoing a major home makeover, I encourage you to tackle your bedroom first. This room can become your haven when the rest of the house is in chaos. Turn your bedroom into the luxurious retreat you were meant to have. Let this chapter be your inspiration to create a place where you can escape, where the rest of the world just melts away.

A Soothing Sanctuary

My bedroom is not just *my* bedroom, to be sure. I jointly share this precious sanctuary with Rob, the love of my life. Images of our individual roots and combined heritage are visible in the bedroom we share more than anywhere else in our home. They serve as reminders to us of the strength of our union. We have surrounded ourselves with what we love. The whole room seems to smile, beckoning us to find repose from any number of intrusions.

From the pictures of those who are closest to us to the soft lighting and smooth sheets . . . our bedroom reflects both our personalities. Make sure yours does, too. As you do, you will begin to be drawn to your own bedroom to rest, rather than feel like it is another room where work awaits.

For that very reason we removed our desk and banished our television set from our bedroom. We just didn't want the intrusion of noise nor work staring at us when we are positioned for pleasure or seeking solitude.

The most important thing to remember when decorating a bedroom is that there is no right or wrong way to go about it. In this most personal room of your house, the only people you need to please are you and your mate.

Most of the fabrics I use throughout my home are mix-and-match checks, textured solids, and stripes coordinated with florals that I love. They combine to bring a soft beauty of God's creation outdoors to the indoors. In our bedroom I find that monochromatic hues and all-white linens create a soothing atmosphere. Whites also bring a sense of spaciousness to a room.

Just adding one or two items that satisfy the touch, feel, and sight, can make any room soothing and pleasurable.

Many manufacturers take the guesswork out of decorating by packaging a variety of ready-made bed ensembles. Then you can opt to add your own personal touches of beautification that makes the room "you." Or reverse your comforter. Then, for a designer touch give your dust ruffle a layered look combining battenburg lace over a color. Echo the battenburg by adding a new pillow or two and gather battenburg as a valance over the top of colored curtains at your windows. (I easily turned a tablecloth into a valance!)

"Eclectic" Decorating Magic

Just this morning I implemented the oldest trick in the decorating rule book — start with what you have! Brand new looks can be created without adding so much as one new item or piece of furniture if you simply move things around.

By reversing the comforter on my bed, interchanging two pictures from a wall to a shelf, arranging a vase of misshapen flowers, and nudging both nightstands in closer to the bed — you could probably have heard my shriek of delight next door! In less time than it takes to make up a bed, I felt like I had invented a more pleasing look. From familiar to fabulous! You can do the same. Or if you have a newly acquired lamp, gift item, or piece of furniture, don't just deposit it in your bedroom.

Take a few moments and let those creative juices flow. See how you can dress up your same ol', same ol'. Come nightfall, you and your spouse will appreciate the alteration. Goodbye to boorrrring!

Whatever your decorating style: sleek, cottage cozy, fashionable, dramatic, formal Victorian, down-home country, or like my style — "eclectic," decorate your home with what brings *you* pleasure. I love the term "eclectic" because it encompasses a broad range of whatever brings me pleasure in decorating. When a particular color scheme, texture, and fabric combination, or piece of furniture "works," I don't have to know *why.* It just works for me!

Pillows are some of the items that "work" for me. A couple of lace pillows add a touch of romance to the casual floral comforter in our bedroom. They echo the curtains which hang adjacent to the bed. Hoffman's rule of thumb: the more throw pillows, the better (especially in the bedroom)!

Pillows are a perfect way to dress up your bed; they make it inviting and interesting. Rob must ask me at least once a week while making or stripping down the bed, "Are you sure we really need all these pillows?" I fervently answer, "YES!!!"

Pillows seem to whisper to me "crawl in and find comfort" in or on my bed. Quilted shams with various shapes, sizes, and colors of throw pillows beautify the bed like nothing else can. Sometimes I simply nestle in stillness among them, letting my spirit be renewed.

It is there that often I will read or write in my journal, just enjoying the quiet for comfort to my soul. These 15 minutes provide for me an intermission in my day. With my heart nourished, my body cannot help but be notably enriched. I'm able to press on for whatever the rest of the day might bring.

The word "eclectic" by definition indicates items are chosen "from various sources." One doesn't need sets of things in matching fabrics or designs. Just adding one or two items that satisfy the touch, feel, and sight, can make any room soothing and pleasurable.

In today's home where every inch counts, bedrooms aren't just for sleeping anymore. They have evolved into retreats that combine sleeping quarters with spa-like baths. Consider using the same soothing tones, patterns, and linens in an adjoining bathroom for a coordinated look of continuity.

Right now, think about what you love to be surrounded by in your home. What puts you at rest? What makes you sigh, "Ahhh," when you see a designed bedroom in a magazine? Use those creative ideas as inspiration in your bedroom decorating.

Bedtime Beauty

Don't restrict your restful touches just to the bed itself! By all means, don't forget the candles — as essential in the bedroom as those pillows! Always have them within reach! I have a pretty basketful of all shapes and sizes in our linen closet. They serve to scent the closet and are easy to fetch at a moment's notice.

Top off your moments of rejuvenation or "power naps" with soft music and candlelight. An adequate setting for relaxation is essential to the enjoyment of your bedroom, yet it is an element that is often overlooked. After all, shouldn't your own comfort and pleasure be as important to you as that of your guests? The answer is a resounding yes! Once you find comfort in your own life, you can face the world a more peaceful you. Everyone wins.

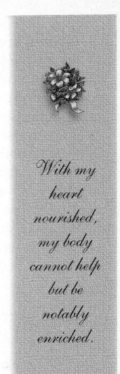

With my heart nourished, my body cannot help but be notably enriched.

Customize your room with adequate lighting for the obvious getting-ready-for-the day routine. Lighting must be bright enough, of course, to match clothing and check hemlines. But, I like to put low-watt lamps on the nightstands for a soft glow. Not only are they a delightful decorator's touch, but they provide light for late-night reading.

Candlelight adds a serene glow and warms the heart. I have recently added candles in various heights and widths cloistered on a mirrored tray atop my dresser. It's an idea I enjoyed in a bed-and-breakfast stay recently. Such a lovely touch of extra ambiance and atmosphere!

You can also find little hurricane covers to give your candles of any height a new look. I just love the new crystal bobeches that are appearing everywhere now in gift stores. These slip down over the tapers and give a mini-chandelier look. Yet another look is the tiny shade that slips over a brass form. I especially like their "quaintness" in florals or brass.

Tuck votives or column candles into virtually *anything*. . . don't just stick to candlesticks. I like to snap up small china plates, trays, and wooden dowels when antique shopping. They make such charming candle creations. Tassels, ribbons, and rosettes brighten the base or mid-point of any taper.

Be as versatile as the ever-changing seasons by using small pumpkins, fresh fruit, pine cones, or yule logs as candle bases. One of the favorite attractions that grace our

Thanksgiving table are some hollowed-out gourds and pumpkins that hold all sizes of candles. After the holiday meal, they are fun to use as clever decorative touches in the bedroom. If you are ambitious you can spray paint the vegetables, glue colored leaves at the base, and place them throughout the house.

For an instant romantic glow to bedroom lighting, I drape a pink nightie over a small lamp that has a pink-tinted bulb. I really enjoy the warm, pleasing visual effect . . . and we all know that any woman is more beautiful by candle-light.

The less clutter, the more the room peacefully summons you to wrap yourself in comfort.

To keep a subdued glow if you think you are going to let yourself actually fall asleep, don't light a candle. Install recessed lighting or use the small lamp on a bed stand. Or you might make a promise to yourself like I have . . . that in my next home I will have a dimmer switch placed in the bedroom to vary the lighting overhead. (Hmm . . . we'll see!)

Suite Dreams

Suite is a wonderful word to use for your bedroom retreat. It is a "sweet" reminder that you enter here for joy and love and laughter.

Little luxuries can enhance the sweet appeal of your current bedroom without a total makeover. Remember, the less clutter, the more the room peacefully summons you to wrap yourself in comfort. Just entering the room can alter your mood. Anxiety, stress, and even anger will be assuaged by the calm atmosphere you establish.

Try picking a bright shade for walls instead of choosing white or cream. Go for a color that makes a strong statement, but has a soothing effect. Good choices are moss green, periwinkle blue, buttery yellow, or coral. If you start with a bright color (green), add one complementary color (blue) and one neutral color (white). This is a foolproof plan where you can never go wrong!

The trick to making a small room look comfy, not crowded, is sticking with mostly solid-colored linens and upholstery. I then like to add touches of simple or whimsical patterns in moderation for interest without making the room look too busy.

"Come to me, all you who are weary and burdened," He beckons. "I will give you rest," says our Lord (Matt. 11:28). Those are not just platitudes, but sound practical advice for all of us. He knows we need regular periods of rest or we will exhaust ourselves, ending up weary, sick, and sidelined.

Perhaps one of the most treasured of items in my own bedroom is a worn, yet luxurious, handmade quilt that rests folded at the foot of my bed. It was presented to me after speaking at a mother-daughter event with a quilt theme. True, its colors enhance my decorating scheme, but the quilt's truest function is to invite me to "come away for awhile." It is especially snuggly on chilly days or cold winter nights — feels like a big, soft hug.

And it does just that. Many are the days I put it to the test! Trying to "get life together" amid each day's heavy issues is a near impossible task without time for refueling for our body and spirit.

Renewal on the run does not bring peace to the soul. In this push-a-button, microwaveable world we live in, it does one good to remember that there are still some things that cannot be fixed by the push of a button. The soul is one of those things!

Give yourself that much-needed time out. Late in the afternoon I can often be found cuddled between my bed comforter and quilt, blanketed in warmth and comfort. Even ten minutes does me wonders! I am a much "happier camper" after even a few restful moments of recline. Resting on top of the bedspread, not in between the sheets, my entire bed does not get askew. Just a quick tidying of my quilt, then I'm ready to face the rest of the day or evening's activities.

Home "Rest"-oration

Inestimable is the comfort provided to a home's spirit when mom and children regularly schedule a restful time-out at some point in the day. How well I can remember those days! When Missy and Mindy were preschool age, if at all possible, I arranged at least one-half hour of quiet time. We all benefited! The practice came from watching a noticeable difference while counseling at summer camp for children. A siesta was built right into each day's schedule as a code. No rest time, then that camper was not permitted to swim or partici- pate in sports for the rest of the day. The consequences were straightfor- ward and fair.

I allowed Missy and Mindy to look at books, soft sing-along tapes, color forms, stickers . . . special quiet activities brought down from the closet shelf solely for this special hour in the day. Just so they stayed reclined on the bed. Children do not have to be sleeping to be resting and clearly every child is not going to actually sleep while napping. But, they will be rest- ing — whether they realize it or not.

Setting the tradition is a good one for it provides a prac- tical separation from other siblings who might be getting grouchy. Or from a mom who might be getting growly! Not long ago I read about the small fry who said, "I didn't get up on the wrong side of the bed this morning, Mommy. I just got up on the wrong side of you!"[3]

I have not met a mother of toddlers yet who could not use a break from the pressures upon her at some point in the day. It may take a week or so of you lying down with your little one reading to him, singing, or talking softly. For our family, these became priceless moments and precious memories we still share today.

If you gasp at the thought, try it before you knock it. With unflinching authority issue the idea as something "for you." It cannot be presented as a recommendation, but as a regimen. No matter how many protests your kiddoes wail, stick it out. Refuse to be drowned in the sea of whining!

Often Missy and Mindy would fall asleep on their own, even after I had told them, "You don't have to go to sleep." I would rest with them, read, or gently get up and accomplish tasks that were waiting.

I am such an advocate of this daily time of comfort for both mom and child. There is no doubt that it is easier to give in to a willful toddler than it is to implement the disciplines of life. I know! I know! It sounds easy on paper, but it is tough to apply to everyday life. I have had trouble following this advice, too. But we can at least *try* to provide what our kids need from us. If we model discipline in our own lives, our children will be much more apt to have self-control when they are grown.

I've been speaking to large groups for well over a decade. In that time I have never met a woman whom I would consider to be inwardly peaceful who doesn't carve out some quiet time for herself in virtually every day. It helps the day to be much more manageable.

I talk to women who complain they have "no time for quiet." Work out a strategy that works for you . . . sneak in moments all through the day. On the way to pick up children from daycare, pull over for a few minutes and pause before rushing in. Try spending a few moments at the close of the day walking in nature or meditating on Scripture, or simply listening to quiet rather than clicking and whining computers or fax machines.

One final reminder concerning taking a daily time-out, or rest time! My dear friend and mentor, Norma Gillming, made it a practice when her children were young to have each of her four children rest quietly for an hour daily regardless of their protests. One particular day she noticed the hour proceeded without protest, even from her rambunctious twin sons.

It seems they had schemed a way to climb out the bedroom window and escape. Grateful for a time to read, Norma had no inkling of their escapades. That is to say, until Kenny hobbled past the living room doorway with the seat of his pants full of thorns. It seems he had landed flat in a bush below the window containing sharp spines rather than the soft ground for which he was aiming!

When rest time seems to be extending just a little too long — it might be wise to take a peek to see why!

Mini-moments of meditation bring my mind back to "stay" on God.

What's Under Your Covers?

"Shadrach, Meshech, and to bed we go!" I can hear my daddy saying that phrase at bedtime as if I were a seven-year-old child again. We kids knew it was time to hit the sack and loved Daddy's ingenuity in getting us to bed. Going to sleep just wouldn't have been complete without it! Bedtime routines bring sweet security to the whole family, especially for children.

Dropping off to sleep may not always be immediate, no matter how exhausted you are. Basic principles of rest include ways to nurture the soul as well as your body. God's presence is a haven for rest.

If time does not permit actually lying down for a reprieve, I look for moments throughout my day to re-focus my heart on God. Mini-moments of meditation bring my mind back to "stay" on God. Rest follows — both in my heart *and* my body.

Right before I rise and just before dozing off at night, in the car, blow-drying my hair — they can all be times for a time of resting in Him. I love to go on long walks down our nearby country road past the cornfields and savor God's presence. I use this time to submerge in the Word. I have found the best fat-free M and M's in the world — meditation and memorization! I use these times to focus on God and to think through my life from His perspective.

First thing in the morning I like to claim a Scripture as "mine for the day." It is often from a passage I'm reading or from a perpetual calendar for that date. A phrase or a verse sticks in my mind and repeats in my heart to apply to my life. As my heart is drawn to Christ in dependence and worship through the day, the verse often takes on a whole new meaning and application.

At the close of the day, I let the reverberant sound of Scripture echo once again in my heart. No one is able to think two thoughts at one time. Try it — you simply can't do it. Our minds are like a television set; only one channel can be viewed at a time! If our inner lives are nourished by what is lovely, our outer lives cannot help but be better.

When you lower those covers at night, lower your stress level as well. You'll find that if you catch yourself tucking problems into bed *with* you, they don't escape outside the covers. They just cover you all night long. If you think something little taken to bed won't matter . . . you've never been to bed with a mosquito under the covers!

Pillow Talk

Being in the ministry means dealing daily with the heavy issues of life. Illness, death, broken homes and marriages, wayward children, and all manner of heartaches might be at the other end of our phone line at any time of any day.

For those reasons Rob and I make it a practice to spend the last hour of the day unwinding. We find it necessary to shut out the cares of the world and let go of the day's burdens. We might read, listen to soft music while gliding on the porch swing together, or relax watching late night TV with a big bowl of popcorn between us (low-fat, of course!).

We have done this for so long now, even when we weren't empty-nesters, that when one of us is traveling the other can retreat and still feel in touch with the other. Lying on the bed to read and await the nightly ritual of a phone-in report, we still feel in sync as if we were together. When I am the absent one, I can visualize Rob in his place as we catch up long-distance on the day's events.

Late night chats are not the times to refer to which major appliance broke that day or the latest digs in an ongoing gripe session with your mother-in-law. Spending winding-down time before retiring with your family members and/or spouse helps to balance the noise and confusion that infiltrates each of our lives virtually every day.

"All night long on my bed I looked for the one my heart loves," Solomon wrote (Song of Sol. 3:1). Quietly, in the comfort of your haven, you can retreat from the world and seek to know the one you married. Listen to his heart, his dreams, his disappointments, and his fears. As you share your time and your hearts in your private retreat you will grow in love and appreciation for each other.

You can fill the bedroom not just with comfortable, interesting items and furniture but with "rare and beautiful treasures," as Proverbs 24:4 says.

In the years ahead, the walls of the room you share can give back sweet memories. Memories of love instead of anger; times of joy and laughter rather than gloom and regret.

Love Nest or Ruffled Nest?

Over the years, there were often times when Rob and I needed a private place for discussion away from Missy and Mindy, regardless of their age. Our bedroom seemed the obvious choice, but really was not a good one. Hashing out discipline problems, budget differences, and family heartaches can put a pallor on your would-be love nest. We decided not to make our peaceful place of rest a place for heated, emotional, or heavy discussion.

Even the best mattress can't provide restful sleep in a war zone! A bouquet of flowers on the dresser is never enough to eradicate the lingering scent of anger and resentment before bedtime. I encourage you not to use your bedroom for weighty subjects. Your bedroom is to be a soothing sanctuary — not a conference room or an emotional baggage terminal!

If your house is small and you have nowhere else to go, try the bathroom. Kids standing outside the door calling, "I need in there!" will help you resolve matters more quickly. Or, like one lady told me, her solution is to "haul the problem out to the garage like garbage." A long walk outside is a great solution when we find ourselves really going at it tooth and toenail over painful issues.

Start over today; decide from this time on, when you must discuss difficult issues that you will go to an "away" area. Having selected a place, be it the basement, the study, garage, attic, or outside, you can determine that voices raised in hurtful words will not be uttered in the bedroom.

Perfume the Sheets

Do you have a fragrance that elicits sweet memories from your past? The sense of certain smells instantly takes me back to places in time. Maybe it's the perfume I wore when I was dating or perhaps a pleasant floral that I recall from when Carolyn and I were college roommates walking back to campus after Sunday church in the spring. Or that lazy, hazy summer smell on a humid evening that reminds me of riding a bike endlessly as a child.

Lay the groundwork for a restful sleep by sprinkling a light powder or spraying a fresh sprit of cologne on your mattress pad or sheets. My favorite is a spray I received as a gift in the Philippines. Pulling back the spread, catching a whiff . . . it carries me back to the memories of that splendid trip. It kind of reminds me of the gardenia flower that was in a special corsage that Rob gave me in college, too.

Your bedroom is to be a soothing sanctuary

When you count the amount of hours you sleep, the bedroom is the place in your home where you actually spend the most of your time. Fragrance makes it interesting, even distinctive. I love the scent of lilacs and was thrilled at the fresh bouquet of them Rob picked for me this spring. I have found a sachet to hang in our closet that is as endearing as those fresh-picked flowers. Now, opening my closet at the beginning and end of each day, I feel instantly tender toward Rob when I'm met with the distinctive lilac fragrance. It seems to have the same effect on him.

Vanilla is a soothing scent that sweetens your dreams, closet, or lingerie drawers. Bedding is the perfect place to add those little touches of scented oils for sumptuous and soothing sleep.

Rest well, my friend. Rest in the shadow of God's precious winds. Instead of counting sheep . . . you can talk to the Shepherd. So shall you then find true rest. Meditate on Him in the night watch. By simply saying "peace be still," any storm in your heart can be calmed. He will never leave you nor forsake you. Remember His words . . . and rest well.

PERSONAL OR GROUP STUDY GUIDE • WEEK 3

1. What a privilege it is that God has given to me the incredible opportunity to be the keeper of a home! How does Proverbs 24:3 say we can fill the rooms of our home with beautiful and rare treasures?

2. Besides material possessions, what rare and beautiful treasures fill your home?

3. Let's get control of our closets this week. Choose one in your home to clean. Now, choose one to let God clean in your heart. (Read Mic. 7:17–18.) Which secret closets are stealing your joy? (Read Ps. 103:12.)

4. Whom in your life will you choose to be excited about their dream and goals this week? How can you enthusiastically cheer him/her by unselfishly giving of yourself in a tangible way?

5. God offers us the gift of salvation, freedom, and life. Have you accepted this gift? Consider (or discuss) how receiving this gift brings great peace and joy.

6. To have "sweet dreams," you can add some restful touches to your bedroom this week. Right now, decide what those will be. (Think: lighting, pillows, scent, nightstand reading, candles, and other little relaxing luxuries.) Share your ideas with the group.

PARAGRAPH PRAYER
Finish writing this paragraph prayer of salvation if you have never made this decision: Lord Jesus, I admit I have known about you for a long time, but have not known you personally. I have lived according to my own rules and religious rituals and I realize I need you. I repent. I want you, Lord, and now receive you into my life. _____

_____

_____

Lovingly,
Your (brand new) Daughter

Come Home to Hope

Close Couple's Comfort Kit

"You love your husband very much, don't you?" I was asked one day after speaking at a workshop. Thinking about the day I stood in pure white at the altar as a bride, I answered an effervescent "YES!"

When Rob and I married 27 years ago, we committed to be faithful to each other and we have been. We promised to love one another with all our heart. And we have tried. Early on, we became aware that we both had much to learn about love — the real kind of love.

By the grace of God and armed with His strength, Rob and I have found that true love means giving ourselves to one another as Christ gave himself to us. That is, each putting the other's welfare and happiness above our own.

The Comfort Every Woman Craves

Psychologists tell us that a woman's most basic need is to feel secure love. This is the foremost comfort every woman craves in marriage. I've never met a woman who doesn't. Next to warm sexual love, a man needs admiration and approval. If your husband's coals of love have been dormant for a long time, it may take more than a spark to re-light his fire of love for you . . . especially if he's been burned before. But, it is possible.

How simple it would have been for Rob and I to go to a bookstore and come home with a manual containing master blueprints for our marriage. We would have followed the plan step by step. But there was no such book. That's no big surprise to anyone, now is it?

So, when our marriage had many more downs than ups during the eighth year, we had to admit we weren't doing well. On the course we were heading, there would not have been a "ten years from now." Something had to be done.

I didn't want a marginal marriage; I wanted the best. I made a conscious decision that something had to be done — and I knew it had to start with me.

I studied; I counseled; I became aware of the differences between the sexes. I read at night until I was cross-eyed. As I began to live by the principles I was learning, little things began changing. Almost immediately, Rob and I began to smile at each other. Our marriage was actually fun again. Romance returned. I almost felt like we were dating again.

One evening during a fun family time, we all four found ourselves laughing and frolicking on the floor. Catching his breath Rob said, "It's been a long, long time since we've heard a good laugh like that around here."

How sad, I thought with deep pangs of regret. But, I knew it was true. Rob was right, it had been way too long. I became more determined than ever to do something about it! As *I* changed, my husband's attitude toward me changed, too. I could hardly believe the communication and intimacy we began sharing.

My disposition became one of relaxed confidence. I had never enjoyed my marriage so much. Rob began to build shelves for me and do things spontaneously again. As I admired and appreciated his work, he would think up more and more to do for me!

I am so grateful that I came out of that pit of self-pity and into a life that is such a joy and solidly stable. What I learned helped me to change (and continues to do so) from an independent, self-righteous mother and wife, into a new person. I realize now that I certainly had not lost my individuality or identity. I finally found it! Along with comfort and security!

Here it is over 25 years after I began applying the principles I've learned about true love. Just a few months ago, one night as I was drifting off to sleep, Rob nudged me. I asked him what was wrong or if there was something he needed. Pulling me close to him, my mega-man husband whispered, "Just want you to know that I love you and I'm glad you love me." He rolled over and went right to sleep.

Now, maybe your husband wakes you up every night in the middle of a dream just to tell you he loves you, but mine sure doesn't. In the darkness I lay savoring that moment over and over for a long time afterward. Oh, the sweet comfort words of love bring!

Even if your marriage has no yellow warning lights flashing like mine did those first few years, the following "Close Couple's Comfort Kit" can guide you to redo, remake, repair, or remodel any marriage. Essentially, when you begin any home repair, you're on the careful lookout for what needs to be fixed. Do the same with your marriage. You locate the cracks and flaws and do what it takes to fix them. This kit will help you "get it together" or simply keep it together!

Use these tools as principles to rebuild your home. Every mistake has a positive quality in it. The changes in your marriage will be dramatic. You will be thrilled. Your husband will be thrilled! He will even be eager to apply the principles personally when he sees what is happening inside and outside of you. Your marriage can truly come alive . . . that's a promise.

TOOL # 1 — RECOGNIZE THAT *YOU* ARE NOT PERFECT

If you are a woman who truly desires that you and your husband can build a home of comfort, there are some issues in your *own* life that first must be hammered out. Recognize the attitudes and actions in yourself that need to be changed first.

Only when I was willing to admit my individual faults was my marriage relationship able to really change for the better. Trying to overcome selfishness in my own strength just made me want to give up. How hard it is for many of us "good wives" to admit that we are not perfect.

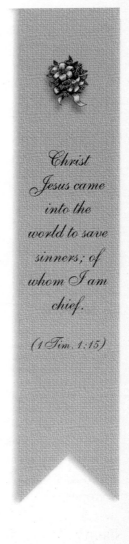

Christ Jesus came into the world to save sinners; of whom I am chief.

(1 Tim. 1:15)

I had always been brought up to be good, kind, and religious. So much so, that it was very humbling to deal with the uncleansed areas of my life. The hard, cold truth was a little threatening, but my pride needed to be broken down.

This first stage takes time. Allow God to bring to your mind any unconfessed sin. Inner change came to me only as I was willing to commit my life to the Lord and ask for His help. I had to learn to agree with Paul when he said, "Christ Jesus came into the world to save sinners — of whom I am the worst" (1 Tim. 1:15), and James, "Humble yourselves before the Lord" (James 4:10). Believe me, it's much easier to humble *yourself* than it is to have God humble you.

In the early years of my marriage I used to think of myself as a loving wife and mother who didn't raise her voice and coped beautifully with difficult situations. Of course, this was not a true perception.

A more realistic observation came from my husband after days when a cloud of tension hung over our home. We went through the motions that everything was fine, but knew it wasn't. There was a barrier between us. The barrier was turning into thick walls.

As weeks turned into years, things got worse. Those walls in our home not only became uncomfortable, they were insurmountable. I wasn't sure what caused them and certainly did not know how to make them go away. But, I knew I didn't like them there. Helpless and un-

happy, I felt up against an enemy I could not define or defy.

In a few short years, I had allowed a negative, critical spirit to permeate my heart and become our home's atmosphere. Staring at the television I felt myself sitting and sighing day after day. I yearned for Rob to take me in his arms as the hero on the tube took the heroine in his.

I felt empty inside. I was afraid to be alone with my thoughts. I longed for something more. What was the answer? I began to search the Scriptures. I knew Jesus said He came to give us abundant life (John 3:34) and that sounded so good to me. I didn't want to just live, I wanted to live abundantly.

This home repair "kit" is not intended to be the ultimate authority on marriage. Far from it. I don't pretend to have automatic, ready-to-wear answers for every marriage problem. I do believe with all my heart that it is possible for almost any wife to revive romance, break down communication walls, and return the sizzle to her marriage. And do so in just a few short weeks' time!

But you must first recognize your own arrogance and pride. Take a long look in your heart's full-length mirror. That's what I did to begin changing my life for the better. We can all profit so much from the beauty that humility brings.

The changes in your own life will bring about change in tangible ways in your husband. Instead of working on him, we must work on *ourselves* first. Backing your mate into a corner of your house would only bring reactions in anger, not actions of love.

Decide if you want to improve your marriage situation. Are you willing to do what God wants for your life, or are you going to continue to redo, redecorate, and remodel your partner? It is really up to you. You are to recognize *your* heart defects, not his!

Is it God's purpose that you have a positive, happy, exemplary marriage as a testimony of His goodness? It sure is! Don't put your faith in a pseudo cure-all or quick fix. Lasting change comes only from above, not from without . . . and it begins with your willingness to recognize that you can't do it by yourself.

Break down barriers by forgiving, apologizing, and most of all — loving.

TOOL #2 — REFRAIN FROM BLAME!

We women rationalize why we *need* to nag, blame, and find fault; after all, isn't all that in our job description? It's like we appoint ourselves to instruct, to remind, to guide . . . sounds more like to "control."

Maybe you are like me. I used to gather up all Rob's faults with the fervor of adding bricks to a stone wall. The walls I built became bitter barricades that only hindered effective communication and affection.

Tear down those walls today! Break down barriers by forgiving, apologizing, and most of all — loving. Because of past bad habits of seeing only negative, you may have to look long and hard to find the good in your mate. Hear me, if you don't . . . there are a lot of other women out there who will!

Even though I have taught these lessons and know them to be true, I still pick up bricks and build walls every now and then. I whine. I compare. I blame. I wail, "How come I'm the only one married to a man who isn't home at 6:00 for dinner every night? Why doesn't someone else at the office go in and check on emergencies that arise? Why does he say he's going to be gone only an hour and then stays gone half the day? How come every other wife has her expectations met?"

Sound familiar to anyone? Whew, with friends like that, what husband needs an enemy? You see how easy it is to find fault? Learn the lesson of "REFRAIN" before it is too late.

My friend who lives nearby tried to "help" her husband for years by criticizing, even often sarcastically saying, "If this situation or trait in you doesn't improve, I just don't think I want to be married to you anymore."

She no longer has to worry. Sadly, they have been divorced a year now. On what would have been her wedding anniversary my friend lamented to me that her greatest regret was being upset and uptight about things that she realized later really didn't matter. She realized too late. But, you don't have to. Refrain from making repeated painful remarks that demean and that kill love.

Thank your Father in heaven for your mate and for the *positive* things you see in him. Philippians 4:8 directs our attention to a checklist of the good in others: "Finally, brothers, whatever is true, whatever is noble, whatever is right, whatever is pure, whatever is lovely, whatever is admirable — if anything is excellent or praiseworthy — think about such things."

No, it isn't easy. But, by an act of your will, you can *choose* to think on the positive in your man. When you read this passage over, can't you find the good things worthy of praise in your husband? Dwell on these things! The way to be happy in any relationship is to let go of the misunderstandings, arguments, or expectations. In five years, is it really going to matter anyway?

Not everything unpleasant that happens in life has to be someone's "fault." We spend our lives wanting people to act a certain way or fit a specific mold and when they're not — we blame, we fight, we hammer at them. I challenge you to go an entire week without any expectations from your spouse. Let go of them! When you free him to be as he is, then you, too, are freed! Free from the binding chains of expecting things to be like the Cinderella Syndrome. Holding on to unrealistic expectations is not true unconditional love.

Marriage was never intended to be a reform school.

Approach this exercise as you would any other. Getting started is the hardest. Remember: place no expectations on your husband. Any at all. Don't expect him to be on time. Don't expect him to be courteous. And guess what? Don't you be surprised when (not if) he is humble, gracious, and kind.

After a week, the exercise gets easier. Your frustration level will lower. Your marriage won't be problem-free, just a lot more fun. Instead of agitated toward each other, you'll both be a lot more accepting of each other. True happiness in marriage comes not when we get rid of all our problems, but when we let go of all our pre-conceived expectations. You will soon discover that marriage can be more of bliss . . . and less of a battle.

Marriage was never intended to be a reform school. If you married your man with the hope of "correcting all his problems," you've been courting a possible disastrous future together. What did not change before marriage is not likely to change at all unless you give him the freedom to change. Maybe it's you who will change . . . you might realize he didn't need to so badly after all!

It's much more important to be kind than to be right!

TOOL #3 — REMEMBER BACK TO WHEN YOU FIRST FELL IN LOVE

Remember what it was about your mate that you fell in love with in the first place? Begin by going back to that moment when you first saw that guy who is now your husband. Where was he? What was he dressed like? How did he act, talk, walk, comb his hair?

Remember? Oh, he was perfect. Not one flaw. You talked on the phone for hours. He held doors open for you. You wrote his name on every piece of paper you could find. You talked about this guy to everyone else constantly. He was your last thought at night and your first thought each morning. You were sure you were falling in love!

Remember what *you* looked and acted like when he first met you? Or how about when he'd pick you up for dates? Remember those long baths and how much time you took getting ready? You met him at the door with powder, perfume, and pizzazz!

Well, what did you look like last night when he came home? Scary thought, isn't it? It's no wonder the honeymoon is over! I'm not saying we gals have be groomed and gorgeous every evening to meet our husbands at the door a la gypsy outfits with beads, bangles, and bare skin.

However, as one man related to me recently, a man does want to come home to a *woman*. That's what he was attracted to when he noticed you in the first place. Femininity. Men are attracted to whatever is the opposite of a man. Femininity is the tender, gentle quality found in a woman's appearance, mannerisms, and nature. Femininity is *accenting* the differences between yourself and men, not the similarities.

It's much more important to be kind, than to be right!

You need not be beautiful to have the charm of femininity. I've known men who think their wives are absolutely beautiful even when a woman is so homely that the fact cannot be overlooked! He's finding her tenderness and loving ways *very* attractive to him. Loud, dominating, slap-you-on-the-back, obnoxious women are not feminine. To a man, they are screamers, unrefined, vulgar, and unattractive.

Analyze your feminine manner. Work on your weak points. Try it for at least a month. Watch how your husband adores you for trying! His natural impulse to provide and protect will be at an all-time high. Femininity sharply defines the difference between men and women, enhancing the attraction one for another.

In the excerpt from a letter that follows, notice how a young wife from Texas fights back sarcasm, aggressiveness, and humiliation:

"I came home from the retreat, and as I looked in the kitchen window, I saw TONS of boxes strewn all over my kitchen . . . the kitchen that I had just worked so hard to get clean the day before retreat. But I remembered your statement about the first four minutes being the most important, and I bit back the frustration and came in the house with a smile and a pleasant (if not totally sincere) hello.

Imagine my surprise when my husband took me by the hand and led me into the living room. Now, having just moved in recently, the living room was the catchall, with boxes almost to the ceiling (literally), and only a small path through them to the couch. So you can imagine how shocked I was when he led me in there, and all the boxes had been unpacked and things were put away, on the walls, etc. I was SO glad that I had kept my sarcastic greetings to myself! He had worked hard all day long trying to have the room finished before I came in, and all that was left was the empty boxes in my kitchen, which he promptly broke down and took out. We were able to have company that night without me being totally embarrassed about the state of my house, thanks to my wonderful husband!"

Thank you, Gina, for sharing with me and letting me use your learned lessons to help others. Gina's response in those first four minutes upon arriving home set the tone for the rest of the evening. She took the retreat advice seriously and it paid off immediately! A heated argument those first four minutes could have put a damper on the whole evening. So it is in the morning when your family gathers to touch base for the busy day. Send your husband off with feminine reminders of peace and harmony.

Remember those endearing qualities about your courtship — the way you were can become the way you *are!*

TOOL #4 — REOPEN THE LINES OF COMMUNICATION

Reopen the lines of communication in your home. A woman expresses her love by words and expects words in return. That's not the way she always gets it. A man more often expresses his love by actions — bringing home the paycheck, sex, buying his wife a house or pots and pans. She wants words and tenderness; he gives her material goods. Is it any wonder that men and women have trouble communicating?

Is your marriage line of communication clogged from under use? It may be shut down to only a few drips a day. You can become a communication plumber and re-open backed-up draining by becoming a good listener. Anyone can talk, but true love really *listens*.

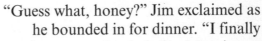

"Guess what, honey?" Jim exclaimed as he bounded in for dinner. "I finally landed the Morris account! What a stress that has been these past two months, but what a relief now."

In the midst of dinner preparation Lynn hastily asked, "Did you remember to pick up the dry cleaning on the way home?" She hadn't heard a word Jim said. He longed for her to be proud of his accomplishment. He was seeking perhaps the one thing that a man needs most from his wife — recognition and respect.

He didn't get it.

Being a sanguine in personality, as well as a speaker by profession, I understand Lynn's predicament. For years I would preoccupy myself when Rob talked or interrupt with a story of my own. I found out, by trial and error, that Rob wants my whole attention. Not half. Not correct or condemn. He wants me to look at him, concentrate on him, hang on every word.

He needs me to be his number one fan and prove it to him by being a good listener. One evening not so long ago before he was to speak at his alma mater, Rob asked me to listen to the message he'd worked so hard on. So I listened. Not just once, but three times I listened to it.

As Rob went through each point, example, quote, I did not sew or look at magazines or file my fingernails. I gave him my undivided attention for almost an hour with my eyes transfixed directly on his. When it came time to present it to the college student body the next morning, I could tell he felt confident. I was thankful I had listened intently. He needed my attention to add affirmation.

Remember something Gary Smalley said in *Love Languages,* "Non-verbal communication is the most powerful part of any message we communicate. Tone of voice, eye contact, facial expressions, show of interest, sincere desire, and patience with the answers."[4]

To me that says that communication is actually listening to the other person's needs as well as what they are verbally saying. It has a lot of everyday practical faces and sounds. I have heard a man say, "Why talk to my wife? She won't even quit doing dishes," or "She's always on the phone when I come home." Message: "I'm insignificant."

I often hear women say, "He just keeps on reading the paper when I tell him about my day," or "I can't unglue him from the TV." Message: "I'm uncherished." Listening, eyeball to eyeball, gives the feeling that "I am on your team and I will help you get where you're going."

The love communicated in greetings and partings is especially important. If you did not experience strong communication bonding in your family of origin, you can start by pausing to take time to greet those whom you have been separated from, let them know that they are important and you are glad to see them again.

Partings are as important as greetings. Make the time to walk your husband to the door as he leaves. Let him know you eagerly await his return. Then stand on the porch waving. (The first time you do this, he may drive back into the driveway thinking you are motioning that he forgot something — my Rob did!) He will leave feeling affirmed and cherished from this enthusiastic parting. He hopes to return home to such a warm and welcoming wife!

Work and schedules are accelerated to the extent that this may not be feasible every single day, but in some way we need to take the time to greet those from whom we've been separated.

I know I am not the most beautiful woman that ever walked the face of this earth . . . or the most talented . . . or the most wonderful, but I sure feel as though I am in Rob's eyes when we are reunited at the end of the day. We communicate. Especially in airports. We communicate! You should see us after a couple days' separation. Deportment goes straight out the window! We cannot restrain the huge smiles across our faces when our eyes meet down that long corridor. I usually jump up and down, expressing sheer glee just to be back together. That's communication!

Is your marriage line of communication clogged from under use?

The "macho" man image is really a myth carried over from the fifties. Contrary to popular opinion, a man doesn't enjoy a knock-down, drag-out fight with his wife. Whether its tears or shouting, he simply does not know how to cope with such emotion. To protect his self-esteem, he fights back.

When I'm mad at Rob, I warn him ahead of time. I say something like, "I'm getting too emotional and growly. I need some time out!" Sometimes I go out on the porch alone, or downstairs to cry and feel sorry for myself. After I calm down and regain my composure, I return to carry on the conversation.

I find that it is best to then say what I have to say; then forgive and forget. Communication is not to sulk, nag, or refuse sex as a punishment. Playing the silent martyr takes too much tremendous emotional effort for me. It only intensifies the problems and turns molehills into mountains anyway. That type of silence is not really golden.

When you communicate by sharing, not shoving, you'll see how easy it will be for your husband to reciprocate. When I built that "wall" of Rob's faults, they became bitter barricades that only hindered effective communication and affection.

Those walls had to come down. By apologizing, forgiving, and — most of all — tenderness, down they came.

If you are like me with past bad habits of seeing only the negative, you may have to work long and hard at finding the good in your husband. If you don't, hear me again . . . there are plenty of other women out there who will!

Oh sure, you will have many opportunities to "correct" your husband. Occasionally I slip back into my old fault-finding ways. When I do, the atmosphere in our home goes *kerplunk*. Everyone ends up being miserable — including me. If I want to spend my time looking at Rob's bad side, I'm sure I can find it. When I spend time criticizing him in my heart, naturally it comes across in my attitude. A woman with a tender, loving heart knows that it is impossible to feel better about herself at the expense of her husband. We've all been uncomfortable around women who have to be "right" all the time. They jump in to correct their husband's story just to prove they know how "it really was."

Just last night I noticed the expression on a man's face as his wife "jumped in there." He stopped talking and let her finish. After all, she obviously was out to prove she was smarter, wiser, and a much better storyteller. The rest of the evening was very uncomfortable. This belittled husband said very little and was clearly embarrassed.

When my conversation focuses on Rob's good, he never tires of hearing it. Neither do I. My critical communication can crush his spirit quicker than anything. It's amazing to me, however, how my positive conversation *to* Rob encourages positive communication *from* Rob. I am keeping a list in my heart of treasures he has said to me in recent months, such as "I love you more and more all the time" and "I sure have enjoyed living with you these 27 years" and "There's honestly no one in this world I'd rather be with than you."

These loving endearments echo in my ears. Just as Rob never tires of hearing how loved he is, neither do I. *That's communication!*

TOOL #5 — RENEW AND REVIVE ROMANCE

Romance, you say, in *my marriage?* What *is* romance, anyway? If we are honest, it has an element of sexual excitement, but is much, much more than that. It's been said that "romance is what makes two married people sit in the middle of a bench when there's plenty of room at both ends."

When you communicate by sharing, not shoving, you'll see how easy it will be for your husband to reciprocate.

What, then, do you do when the romance has gone out of your marriage? Answer: You go right back to the One who created marriage and the beauty of sex. To God. It was His idea in the first place. It is to be guilt-free and wholesome. Sex is God's lovely wedding gift to every bride and groom. What a great romantic!

Sex is not everything in marriage, so I am not trying to exaggerate its importance. But, it is an integral part of the marriage relationship when there is a mating of spirit with spirit. We don't need to be ashamed to talk about what God was not ashamed to create. God conceived the idea by creating the two sexes instead of just one.

Imagine the fun and games Adam and Eve had in the garden. There were no marriage manuals or counselors to consult. Imagine Adam exclaiming, "Where have you been all my life!" (That's a rather loose translation; it was actually, "Bone of my bones, flesh of my flesh.")

God provided someone to meet Adam's needs. There they were — naked, beautiful, perfect, trusting one another. They fit together perfectly! When a relationship is built on standards of trust, commitment, understanding, and unselfish devotion, romance flourishes. If your intimate love life is not all you want it to be, you can do something about it today. It is surprising how uneducated many husbands and wives are concerning sex. In many cases a re-educating about the basics is all that is needed to relieve tension in the romance department.

There are so many good Christian manuals that deal specifically with the physical mechanics of sex that both you and your husband might find helpful. Attitudes that may have affected your sex life for years can be altered with proper wholesome sex education.

PERSONAL OR GROUP STUDY GUIDE • WEEK 4

1. If a fire were consuming your home, what important, precious valuables would you gather? According to Matt. 6:25–34, what wealth would last forever?

2. List the first five tools to re-build marriages in the *Close Couple's Comfort Kit* by finishing these sentences and ask yourself, "Why is this so important?" #1: RECOGNIZE that you are not _____. #2: REFRAIN from _____. #3: REMEMBER back to when you first _____ __ _____. #4: RE-OPEN the lines of _____. #5: RENEW and REVIVE _____!

3. Abigail is a wonderful example of someone who stayed in an unhappy marriage. Read together and discuss 1 Samuel 25:2–42. Visualize yourself in this woman's situation. (See also 1 Cor. 7:10–11.)

4. If "men are from Venus" and "women from Mars," how *do* couples stay married? Ephesians. 5:33b states a practical way a wife can express her love. Ephesians 5:21 describes the sensitivity that should exist between spouses. Ephesians 4:32 tells us how to communicate in a constructive manner.

5. Why do *you* think most people divorce today?

6. Have you ever thought about divorce due to "incompatibility"? Have well-meaning friends and family encouraged you to bail out of your marriage? How has divorce touched your family?

PARAGRAPH PRAYER for the Married Woman
Finish writing this paragraph prayer of unwavering commitment to your marriage: Lord, help me to remember that it's not by my power nor might, but by Your Spirit that anything in my marriage relationship can be re-built for You. Help me to remember the reasons I married my husband in the first place, especially _____

_____
_____

Lovingly,
Your Daughter

PARAGRAPH PRAYER for the Unmarried Woman
Finish writing this paragraph prayer whether you are "waiting or wanting": Lord, help me to grasp how long and high and deep Your love is (Eph. 3:17–19) so that I might focus wholeheartedly on You and not what is missing in my life. Right now, I_____

_____
_____

Lovingly,
Your Daughter

TOOL #6 — RELINQUISH YOUR HUSBAND TO HIS RIGHTFUL OWNER

Your husband will never truly be yours until you have first given him to God. You do not *own* him! He is yours only when you are willing to let him go wherever God calls him and to do whatever God wants him to do!

When I got married I had some preconceived notions of what the future would be. You might say I was bitten by a bug with Cinderella symptoms. This "disorder" leaves one with delusions that hinder the thinking processes. In my case, my thinking was stymied, all right. I dreamed only of living in a white, two-story house on an acre of ground, with tall, rustling trees in the backyard, and flower gardens surrounding the entire setting. There would be soft, fluffy snow in the winter and green fields filled with clover in the summer. Everyone would arrive at our home for the holidays. We'd have a full, long table with turkey and the trimmings.

When I discarded this unrealistic dream I was a happier, better wife. I found that through the years this dream got in my way and made me less adaptable than I should have been. To be adaptable, *make your dreams portable.* Plan to be happy anywhere — on a mountain or in a burning desert; in poverty's vale or abounding in wealth. Why is this so important? Because your husband is not yours.

Don't be rigid and set in your ways. Determine to adjust to life's circumstances. God's ways are not always our ways. A contented spirit during times that require flexibility is a rare quality in a woman. It is, however, a quality that is treasured by men. To be adaptable you have to be unselfish, care more about others than yourself, and put your marriage in top priority. Yes, I discarded my unrealistic dreams but held on to the dreams that I felt were non-negotiable.

And you know what? Many, many of them have come true! *When you cast your bread upon the waters, it comes back to you buttered!* Don't lose sight of what is honestly a God-given goal or dream. But, relinquish people to the One who can make those dreams come true.

Just as Abraham had to open his hands and yield on that ancient altar the one thing that kept him from complete surrender, so we have to yield. Your husband is your husband. Not your possession. His first love is God. Not you. Don't make him choose between you two. The greater the possessiveness, the greater the pain in letting go.

Often we are hindered from giving up our treasures out of fear for their safety or security. But, wait a minute! Isn't everything safe and secure in the hands of God? In fact, nothing or no one is really safe or secure *unless* they are totally committed to God. No child. No dream. No job. No romance. No friend. No house. Especially, no husband.

To be adaptable, make your dreams portable. Plan to be happy anywhere.

What does God want us wives to do? I've had to do it a zillion times. Let go. Release the grip. Turn loose. No matter how you phrase it, it still creates panic and fear in our hearts. "But, my husband is not a godly man and I cannot trust him," you say. God can do a much better work in his life if you step out of the way.

Wise was the older woman years ago who gave me some very good advice when she said, "Sharon, it is your job to make Rob happy; not holy!" It's one of those great paradox lessons. The more I let go of Rob, the more he truly becomes "mine." Mine in love, mine in laughter, mine in life! Like one of those "less is more" admonitions. I've tried clinging . . . Rob just struggles hard to get away. When I release, he seeks me out all the more.

We're told that "whosoever shall *lose* his life shall *find* it." I've had to learn that lesson the hard way, but have found it to be absolutely true.

Can losing actually produce gain?

It sure can! How unpopular that philosophy is today. Somehow people can't handle losing. We just are not taught that losing could be a positive thing.

From our rat-race perspective, it seems that Jesus must have had a few things mixed up. To us, losing is unpleasant. Losing means failure. To us maybe; not to Christ. Many women frantically scurry around looking everywhere for ways to improve intimacy with their husband, when the secret has been right there all along. The secret is in the yielding.

One woman wrote me from Ohio that she and her husband were seriously thinking of separation. They were both miserable. One evening she stopped the packing and started praying. "O God, help me to lose my husband (to You) so I can find him!" What a freedom she discovered in letting go! I love how she concludes her letter, "I took my hands off of my husband, now *he can't keep his hands off me!*"

Of course there was much more to her letter as this young woman told their story, but let me just include the poem entitled "Treasures" — it says it all.

Treasures

One by one He took them from me.
    All the things I valued most
Until I was empty-handed;
    Every glittering toy was lost.
And I walked earth's highways, grieving,
    In my rags of poverty.
Till I heard His voice inviting
    "Lift your *empty* hands to Me!"
    (italics mine)
So I held my hands toward heaven,
    And He filled them with a store
Of His own transcendent riches
    Till my hands could hold no more.
And at last I comprehended
    With my stupid mind and dull
That God could not pour His riches
    Into hands already full.
        by Martha Snell Nicholson[5]

TOOL #7 — RESTORE RESPECT

What is a man proud of? A man needs to feel proud of his masculine role by meeting these five masculine needs:

1. A man needs to be admired.
2. A man needs to know he is appreciated.
3. A man needs companionship.
4. A man needs to be prayed for.
5. A man needs to be affirmed for who he is.

Respect is restored in a marriage when a wife fills her husband's emotional cup with admiration. He needs to hear that you *really need him*. So deep is his need to feel needed as a man and to serve as a man, that when he is no longer needed he may question his reason for living. This affects a man's tender feelings for his wife since his romantic feelings partly arise from her need to be protected, sheltered, and cared for.

Unfortunately, we women too often meet so many of our own needs ourselves that our husbands fail to receive the honor they crave. They long to meet our needs and serve as the protector, sheltering you from harm, danger, or difficulty. Respect is shown to a man by a strong, wise woman who has learned to trust her husband.

Many men will do just about anything to gain the admiration of others, especially their families. They will search and search for someone to love and respect them. *Make sure that someone is you.* Honor his position as the head of the family and teach your children to do so. If you do feel that he is about to make a mess of things, first hear his point of view. Don't hasten to jump in. Spend a lot of time thinking before you step in and advise; then outline a course for him to follow. Not man to man. But, as a woman who loves, respects, and cares.

Let go of the reigns in the family. Turning over rightful control to your husband is extremely important as a basis for couples to achieve a genuinely satisfying relationship in marriage. Follow your husband when he leads. Remember: if we wives would be better followers, many husbands would become better leaders.

Don't expect every decision your husband makes to make sense to you. Sometimes decisions may defy logic. If he is leaning on the Lord concerning a decision and not just trying to be the "big kahuna," ask your Heavenly Father to guide him. If his plans do not make sense to you, nor his judgment appear the least bit sound, perhaps it isn't. But, the ways of God don't always follow logic. God may lead your husband into problems or allow him to even fail for a wise reason. Let God try him in the refiner's fire if He so chooses. And get out of the way! If you don't, *you* will end up getting burnt!

When I step aside and let God do what He so chooses in the lives of those I love, things often turn out right in a surprising way. When Rob senses that I trust his overall judgment and motives, it makes him feel so responsible that he makes sure he does the right thing. Turning things over to him through the years has built my confidence in him and his confidence in himself.

Have faith in the principle that God has placed your husband at the head and commanded you to obey him, as stated in the Bible in Ephesians 5 and 1 Peter 3. The home can only fulfill its true purpose when it is God-controlled. Leave Jesus Christ out of your home and it loses its meaning. But follow Christ's plan for the home, and He will make it the greatest haven this side of heaven. If you can't trust your husband concerning an issue, you can always trust God!

As a wife, doing recreational things with your husband can be a real key to companionship. This doesn't mean you have to take up hunting or basketball, but picking an interest of his can pay rich dividends: walking, swimming, golf, antique hunting, fishing, gardening, refinishing furniture together — just to name a few.

By taking advantage of a variety of ways to participate in activity with your husband, you are showing him that you want to spend time with him. That honors him. That shows respect. Be flexible with your schedule whenever possible instead of saying "I don't want to go" or "I don't have time." We all seem to have time to do what we feel is the most important in life. Your marriage is. It's important to evaluate how we spend our time and what areas we can eliminate in order to schedule quality time with our mate.

Many Christians have mastered the art of looking spiritual and happy on the outside. But once they enter their homes, they take off the masks and let down their guards.

They take out their frustrations on the people who mean the most to them. For many, that frustration is taken out on their spouse so that the children are "spared."

Respect gives your husband permission to be himself. You, as the wife, become the "safe" person to whom he can express himself and know he will be understood, trusted, and not condemned for it. The secret of empowering a man with respect is not trying to change him or improve him. When a man feels loved, trusted, respected, and appreciated — automatically he begins to change, to grow, and to improve in the very areas you desire him to.

Many times I have mistakenly tried to "fix" Rob and he responded by defending himself. The behavior I was trying to fix stayed the same. He did not feel accepted so he actively or passively resisted. He only felt controlled and corrected.

The best way to help a man grow is to let go of trying to change him, and pray, pray, pray. In prayer, I accept Rob's feelings, actions, or "imperfections." Praying to God out loud, if possible, gives me a greater awareness of the truth that God is in control, not me. Rather than disrespect, Rob appreciates my vulnerability and sensitivity when he knows I have taken a matter to the Lord. Remember: Men are more willing to say "yes" if they are respected and know they have the freedom to say "no."

TOOL # 8 — REFUSE TO CHOOSE DIVORCE AS AN OPTION.

The best place to make this choice is before the church bells begin to ring and you're walking down the aisle. Unfortunately, not every couple does. When couples fall in love we feel as though we will be happy forever. We cannot imagine not loving our partner or ever being with someone else. It is a magical time when everything in the relationship is in harmony and works effortlessly.

Then we realize our partner is not as perfect as we thought. We have to work at love, getting along, and daily life. He isn't the man we thought we knew. In fact, he is from another planet! We discover our husband is flawed and makes mistakes. It is no longer easy to give love. Not only is it difficult . . . we do not always feel like giving love.

Love is seasonal. Summertime brings disappointments that must be up-rooted under the hot, sweltering heat of discouragement. Autumn's harvest is golden-rich and fulfilling. A more mature love grows and understands an abundance of hope and possibilities. There are the cold, difficult, barren winters. The weather changes again, and springtime comes. It is a time of relationship renewal and enjoyment of the union that love has created.

We have to work at love, getting along, and daily life.

I have witnessed countless couples who have worked hard through all these seasons, year in and year out. *Commitment* is the common trait that I've observed that infused their marriages through difficulties in each season. Commitment. Strange, isn't it, that it all boils down to one word. Yet that one word is in short supply in many marriages.

We are a culture that is used to getting what we want instantly. We hate waiting patiently — on anything. We can push a button to instantly raise our garage door, open our car, lock our house, cook an entire meal in just a few seconds. We don't want to wait. That takes commitment. There's that word again.

Are you committed? When you go through a difficult season in your marriage, your mate needs to hear words of commitment — not rejection. Each time you argue about a problem or disagree, do you threaten to leave? What a cruel tactic! It instills fear in your husband and erodes the security of your marriage.

Tell your husband how much you love him. Often. Many, many times. Not just in the peaceful seasons, but in the turbulent times. Assure your husband that you will remain loyal and true to the marriage covenant that you agreed to preserve when you said "I do." Never threaten to leave. (The exception here would be if you or your children are in danger of being harmed. Then go to a safe place and get help. Don't become a casualty or statistic. In the case of physical or psychological abuse, homosexuality, drunkenness, drugs, etc., separation may be necessary while searching for a redemptive solution.)

Make sure your husband knows that you are committed to your marriage, especially if you have threatened to leave him in the past. A wedding anniversary would be the opportune time to sweetly and sincerely demonstrate your devotion. Tell your husband that you would marry him all over again! Tell him that the idea of divorce is not even an option to you.

I listened to a dear young husband recently who, through tears, shared with me how his wife had come home and done just that. Weeping in humility and grace he took her in his arms and held her with a tenderness never before. This man's fears of losing his precious little wife were finally put to rest. To put it in his words, "I felt like a plant that had been placed out in the sun after being inside for a long, dark winter."

Don't believe the lies of Satan and society that say you can just marry someone else later if your marriage doesn't work out. Our culture wants you to believe that you can come out unscathed. I wish you could see the tears and heartache that Rob and I have witnessed during marriage break-ups. God shuns divorce. He says so in Malachi 2:15–16. It was never His choosing from the very beginning.

Poor marriages are *caused* by not repairing the home — good marriages are *created* by building with these tools. Yes, you and your husband are in this thing together. If your roof springs a leak, you're *both* going to get wet. And if enough water from the storms of life gets in, you're both going to drown. Either you both win or you both lose. There is no other option. Marriage demands the integrated efforts of both you and your husband.

The very best athletic teams understand that success is built on the strengths of all their players. The burly strongman may make fantastic tackles, but the small, agile player can sneak through the line without getting crunched. Games are won because they have developed a team approach where each player uses their God-given strengths.

So it is that marriage partners know where their strengths lie, as well as their corresponding weaknesses. They compensate for one another; they work together. It's two sides of the same coin. Through any dark season, refusal to even consider divorce as an option helps heal many wounds.

The best thing you can do for your children is to love their father.

One last thought with this tool is something that I heard years ago. It went something like this: "The best thing you can do for your children is to love their father." The trust that you give your husband and your children when you make your commitment known will give your family some precious gifts. Gifts every family longs for: of feeling safe, secure, and strong.

Luke 1:37 tells us, *"For nothing is impossible with God."* You don't have a problem that He cannot work out — if you turn that problem over to God. It doesn't matter how painful your situation is, God cares. Tell Him about it (1 Pet. 5:6–7). Ask Him what to do (James 1:5–8). Be sure that what you think you hear Him say agrees with His written Word (John 8:31–32). Obey Him (John 7:17). Trust Him (Isa. 26:3–4). God won't always do *your* will. But when He doesn't, it is because He will do "immeasurably more than all we ask or imagine" (Eph. 3:20).

Henry Ford was asked on the occasion of his 50th wedding anniversary, "What is the formula for a good marriage?" He replied, "The same as for a successful car: stick to one model." That's great advice, Mr. Ford!

This World Is Not My Home

If I decided to build a house, what would my house look like? On paper, some kind of monstrosity, I'm sure! I would definitely need an architect who could draw not only an overall plan, but an extremely detailed one.

In a small town not too many miles from where I live, a superb home has just been completed. Master builders from all across the Midwest worked one entire year to finish this widely acclaimed home in time for the world's only living septuplets' first birthday. In fact, today is moving-in day for the now-famous McCaughey family. Completion of their home, which is three times the size of an average home, has been quite a feat — even for the most accomplished designers.

To build such a mammoth house required master builders. They had to plan in a most grandiose scale for a home that would meet the needs of seven toddlers who would someday become seven teenagers. Planning right along with the input of the parents, the contractor had to be one very patient builder. They longed for their house to be a place where the children could run, play, and grow up in private. "To be their home, not a museum," pleaded Kenny McCaughey.

I'm sure there are not many human architects anywhere willing to take on a solemn project like that. But that describes the Lord Jesus perfectly. Given complete control, He will build within us each a lovely house indeed! A house will stand the storms of life when Christ is not only our architect and builder, but the foundation as well.

Jesus does not want to just *lay* a foundation, but will *become* the foundation. "For no one can lay any foundation other than the one already laid, which is Jesus Christ" (1 Cor. 3:11). He desires to become the sure, secure foundation in the "ways" of your life.

You both win or you both lose.

So far in this book we've taken your old house, the "real you," and we've done a lot of remodeling and renovating. We've painted, planted some new shrubs, and repaired a few loose shutters on the outside. Inside, we've cleaned closets, dusted throughout, vacuumed under the sofa, and decorated with lovely touches to enhance the comfort level.

What we need now is the power. Without a power source for warmth, light, and air flow, your shell is nothing more than a glorified outhouse. Years ago I "plugged in" to the world's greatest power source. You can, too. Making the connection means abundant life for you. I'd love to show you how.

Opening the Door of Your Heart

Have you ever stood outside a friend's house knocking and ringing the doorbell until finally you left, assuming no one was at home? Jesus stands at the door of your heart today, dear friend (Rev. 3:20). He longs to dwell there through faith (Eph. 3:16–17). He longs to settle down and be at home. Christ will live in any human heart that welcomes him in through believing on Him.

It's your choice. The door of your heart represents that power of choice. No matter what sin or what pain there might be in your past, Jesus is ready to forgive and to make you whole (1 John 1:9). The love of Christ is clear in many passages in the Bible, perhaps the dearest in John 3:16: "For God so loved the world that he gave his one and only Son, that whoever believes in him shall not perish but have eternal life."

Oh, God's love for me! I never get over it. I hope I never do. Jesus said he came to give us an awesome, abundant life (John 10:10). But how do you plug into the power of the God of the universe? Thousands of years ago, Isaiah said, "Your iniquities have separated you from your God" (Isa. 59:2). Our sins, yours and mine, keep us away from God and his power. Oh, you may not feel like the "bad" in your life is too bad. I didn't either until I came across the truth in the Bible that astounds me.

They weren't gross sins, but I was guilty of them nonetheless. Worry, pride, gossip, and unbelief, to name a few. That was me . . . separated from God due to the fact that the penalty for sin is spiritual death according to Romans 6:23. But, there's good news, too, right in the same verse: "But the gift of God is eternal life in Christ Jesus our Lord."

Since I knew I could not personally bridge the wide gap to God by myself, that *is* good news. Great news! What's more, the Bible tells us how to accept that gift of eternal life. The verses in Ephesians 2:8 and 9 read, "For it is by grace you have been saved, through faith — and this not from yourselves, it is the gift of God — not by works, so that no one can boast."

Jesus spent a lifetime on this earth unselfishly healing broken lives and broken hearts. He then died so that we might live. He stands knocking at a symbolic door of our heart: "Here I am! I stand at the door and knock. If anyone hears my voice and opens the door, I will come in and eat with him, and he with me" (Rev. 3:20).

By faith, I opened my heart's door to Jesus when I was just a young child. For nearly 40 years, His free gift has been the source of my peace and joy. I am His very own child, spiritually born into the family of heaven with the promise of a heavenly home. Forever secure because of what Christ has done for me, there is not a chance of losing my eternal life because it has been paid for and secured by what Christ did on the cross.

When a friend comes to your home with a special delivery, you can hardly wait to let him in. Now Jesus is asking to come into your heart as Lord and Savior. He stands knocking with a gift of incomparable value — that gift of eternal life! Won't you let Him come into your heart and life right now? If you believe that He died as the Savior for the sins of the world, invite Him in today.

Your Heart Becomes a Home

There are two kinds of redecorating. Don't be satisfied with a new outer paint job and some temporary redoing. Remodel from the ground (heart) up! Receive, accept the One, the only One, who can bring true comfort and give you life. Pascal once said, "There is a God-shaped vacuum in the heart of every man, which cannot be satisfied by any created thing, but only by God, the Creator." God is waiting and wanting to fill the vacuum of your heart.

The gift of God is eternal life in Christ Jesus our Lord.

(Rom. 6:23)

Right now your heart can become a heart of confidence, calm, and comfort . . . instead of chaos. Jesus Christ promises these wonderful benefits to all who open their heart's door to Him. Invite Him into your life. Simply open the door. The following is a suggested prayer that many women in my classes have used:

> Dear Jesus, I need you. Thank You for loving me so much that You died on Calvary's cross. Right now, I open the door of my heart to invite you into my life as my personal Savior. I ask You to forgive my sins and make me the kind of person You want me to be. I love You, Lord, and I thank You. Amen.

I give you my word, dear reader, when you give your heart and life to Christ, there is no greater comfort to be found! Christ IS the great comforter. He alone will give the peace that I, too, had searched for all too long. He promises to settle in and be at home as the Lord of your heart. It's as though you transfer the title and deed over to Jesus Christ. Sign it over.

You will never be the same. You will never be sorry.

Transfer of the Title

As owner and master of my heart, Christ has the freedom to manage and operate my life as He chooses. It is no longer my responsibility to keep my heart what it ought to be. I couldn't live a pleasing Christian life in my own strength. It would be impossible. The only way it really works is to give Christ full ownership — for time and eternity. God's Word assures me that He holds the deed to my heart firmly

in His hands. Giving Him daily control makes sure that I do not take it back! He can do a much better job of taking care of my assets and liabilities than I ever could anyway.

The gift of salvation is not the last gift God offers us. It's the first. And it sets the pattern for all that follow.

Salvation from sin's guilt is only the beginning. Look at all the other gifts He has freely bestowed upon us as His children.

First of all, I have *confidence* — the inner confidence that comes from God Himself. God has given us all we need to be confident. "God did not give us a spirit of timidity, but a spirit of power, of love and of self-discipline" (2 Tim. 1:7).

I am confident that I am never alone because God has said, "Never will I leave you; never will I forsake you" (Heb. 13:5).

I am confident that He will always provide for me. "I was young and now I am old, yet I have never seen the righteous forsaken or their children begging bread" (Ps. 37:25).

I am confident that I can make it through whatever life brings my way for "I can do everything through him who gives me strength" (Phil. 4:13).

I am confident in my relationship with Christ, "I know whom I have believed, and am convinced that he is able to guard what I have entrusted to him for that day" (2 Tim. 1:12).

I am confident that I can trust God implicitly to be at work in my life. "My grace is sufficient for you, for my power is made perfect in weakness" (2 Cor. 12:9).

I am confident that I can rely on God, no matter what. "In quietness and trust is your strength" (Isa. 30:15).

I can do everything through him who gives me strength.

(Phil. 4:13)

Secondly, I have a *calm* that I can live in safety and without fear. "Do not fear, for I am with you; do not be dismayed, for I am your God, I will strengthen you and help you; I will uphold you with my righteous right hand" (Isa. 41:10).

> *I have a calm* during the storms of life for God has promised, "When you pass through the waters, I will be with you; and when you pass through the rivers, they will not sweep over you" (Isa. 43:2).
>
> *I calmly do not* have to be afraid when others attack me. "The Lord is a refuge for the oppressed, a stronghold in times of trouble" (Ps. 9:9).
>
> *I can know a calm* and quiet in this noisy world. "Whoever listens to me will live in safety and be at ease, without fear of harm" (Prov. 1:33).
>
> *I can calmly* face the future. " 'For I know the plans I have for you,' declares the Lord, 'plans to prosper you and not to harm you, plans to give you hope and a future' " (Jer. 29:11).
>
> *I can feel calm* when I feel like I'm going to lose my mind! "And the peace of God, which transcends all understanding, will guard your hearts and your minds in Christ Jesus" (Phil. 4:7).
>
> *I have an unexplainable calm* that nothing in this world can offer, for Jesus said, "Peace I leave with you; my peace I give you. I do not give to you as the world gives. Do not let your hearts be troubled and do not be afraid" (John 14:27).

Thirdly, I have unlimited *comfort* available to me. To belong to the Creator of the world, what could be a greater comfort? He knows me, sees me, cares for me, and loves me! (Ps. 147).

> *I have comfort* because the comforter actually lives within my heart. "And I will ask the Father, and he will give you another Counselor to be with

you forever — the Spirit of truth. The world cannot accept him, because it neither sees him nor knows him, But you know him, for he lives with you and will be in you" (John 14:16–17).

What comfort to know that God is in control. He's omnipotent, having all power (Luke 1:35); omnipresent, everywhere present at the same time (Psalm 139:7); and omniscient, all knowing (1 Cor. 2:10–11).

Comfort is mine when I am broken-hearted. "The sacrifices of God are a broken spirit; a broken and contrite heart, O God, you will not despise" (Ps. 51:17).

My heart is comforted when I realize that I am going to be with Jesus in my heavenly home eternally. "We are confident, I say, and would prefer to be away from the body and at home with the Lord" (2 Cor. 5:8).

I am comforted in any circumstance when I feel like everything or everyone is against me. "If God is for us, who can be against us?" (Rom. 8:31).

I can think of nothing more comforting than realizing God is with me always. "Never will I leave you; never will I forsake you" (Heb. 13:5).

I find comfort in knowing that God's plan is not for me to fail, but to succeed. " 'For I know the plans I have for you,' declares the Lord, 'plans to prosper you and not to harm you, plans to give you hope and a future' " (Jer. 29:11).

Do not let your hearts be troubled and do not be afraid.

(John 14:27)

Comfort is available during excruciatingly painful and trying times in my life. "And we know that in all things God works for the good of those who love him, who have been called according to his purpose" (Rom. 8:28).

I am secure and comforted in accepting the love of Christ. "Who shall separate us from the love of Christ? Shall trouble or hardship or persecution or famine or nakedness or danger or sword? . . . No, in all these things we are more than conquerors through him who loved us. For I am convinced that neither

death . . .

   life . . .

      angels . . .

         demons . . .

            present . . .

               future . . .

                  powers . . .

                     height . . .

                       depth,

                         nor anything

else in all creation, will be able to separate us from the love of God that is in Christ Jesus our Lord" (Rom. 8:35–39).

PERSONAL OR GROUP STUDY GUIDE • WEEK 5

1. Review the remaining three tools to rebuild marriages in the *Close Couple's Comfort Kit* by finishing these sentences and discussing why this "tool" is essential in a marriage relationship:

#6 RELINQUISH your husband to his _____ _____.
#7 RESTORE _____.
#8 REFUSE to choose_____ as an option when getting married.

In what type of situation is one justified in deciding to leave or disobey authority? (See Acts 4:18–20). Even among noted biblical students and pastors, disagreement exists on the subject of divorce and remarriage. Carefully read and study the following passages to develop a personal perspective on the subject:

Malachi 2:16   Genesis 2:24   Matthew 19:1–9
Mark 10:1–12   Romans 7:1–3   1 Corinthians 7:12–15

2. If you or someone you know is recovering from a divorce, let these verses be a guide for removing guilt, healing, and a healthy "moving on." John 4:16–18 — Jesus offered a fresh start and forgiveness to the woman at the well. We must respond in the same Christ-like manner.

3. "The very best thing you can do for your children is to love their father." How is this statement true and why is it so vital in the 21st century?

4. According to Ephesians 2:20 who/what should be the cornerstone of our home?

5. Taking our eyes off of ourselves and focusing on others brings restoration. Once again, relationships become alive, fresh, and vibrant! Replace your own name in the blanks below paraphrased from 1 Cor. 13:4–8: _____ is patient, is kind, does not envy, does not boast, is not proud, is not rude, is not self-seeking, is not easily angered, keeps no record of wrongs, does not delight in evil but rejoices with the truth. _____ always protects, trusts, hopes, perseveres. _____ never fails.

PARAGRAPH PRAYER
Finish writing this paragraph prayer of personal worship: Father God, thank You for Your power. Enable me to make the right choices in every part of my life, especially today in the areas of _____
_____
_____
_____

Lovingly,
Your Daughter

Homesick For Heaven!

When our Missy was away at college the first semester, she was so homesick that the daily calls shot our phone bills sky-high. By the time Thanksgiving arrived our family couldn't wait to be all together again. Homesickness hurts. As Missy's mom, I felt it . . . badly. You know the kind of pain . . . that way-down-deep kind. It was the kind that makes me want to just sit and moan. It's similar to an impending "all-day morning sickness nausea" weary feeling! You can't really explain what's wrong, you just know something is not right.

A week before Missy's holiday break that first fall, something happened to all of our family. Our spirits rose daily. I ceased my "groaning" because I knew that soon we would all spend the next few days with the ones we love the most in this world.

Missy's phone conversations turned from despair to effervescence and encouragment. "I can make it now," she'd exclaim, "I'm coming home soon!" When I saw that little beige car turn into the driveway of our modest house on the corner lot, I dropped whatever I was doing. I hugged that girl long and hard. Both of us were no longer homesick.

You and I can "make it" even when life doesn't run smoothly. We, too, have the hope of going home soon!

Sometimes God deliberately builds hassles and heartache into each of our lives to help us keep our eyes on our eternal home rather than on our earthly one. He is preparing a place for His redeemed more glorious than we can ever imagine.

The Best Home Show Ever

Human imagination can not comprehend the beauty of the believer's eternal paradise. It would be impossible to imagine the splendor we will behold when we first arrive on location. We do know that heaven is a huge and colorful place, but that is not as important, in the final analysis, as the fact that we will live forever there with God.

The Bible does not tell us every detail of our eternal home. What we do know is that everyone who has received Christ as personal Savior has become a child of God (John 1:12) and now possesses eternal life in heaven (John 5:24). The central focus of heaven will not be the walls, streets, or gates, but rather the Lamb of God and His throne.

John noted a beautiful emerald green rainbow surrounding the throne (Rev. 4:3). In verse 6 he cited, "Before the throne there was what looked like a sea of glass, clear as crystal."

Heaven will be spotlessly clean and built of transparent gold. The city itself is surrounded by a wall of jasper, as beautiful as a crystal clear diamond, and as brilliant as a transparent icicle in bright sunshine (Rev. 21:18).

With its main street paved with pure gold, heaven's walls rest on 12 foundations inlaid with various precious stones (Rev. 21:18–21). You and I have toured some magnificent homes before; I've been honored to stay in some bed and breakfast homes that were breathtaking upon arrival. But, oh, dear friend, heaven's colorful elements form a beauty never known to our human eye. Even the finest home shows have not come close to the grandeur we will behold!

What Heaven Is:

Heaven is indescribable: "However, as it is written: No eye has seen, no ear has heard, no mind has conceived what God has prepared for those who love him" (1 Cor. 2:9).

Heaven is incredible: "He will wipe every tear from their eyes. There will be no more death or mourning or crying or pain, for the old order of things has passed away" (Rev. 21:4).

Heaven is instantaneous: "After that, we who are still alive and are left will be caught up together with them in the clouds to meet the Lord in the air. And so we will be with the Lord forever" (1 Thess. 4:17).

Heaven is ingenious: "Now we know that if the earthly tent we live in is destroyed, we have a building from God, an eternal house in heaven, not built by human hands" (2 Cor. 5:1).

Heaven is individual: "Jesus said to her, 'I am the resurrection and the life. He who believes in me will live, even though he dies; and whoever lives and believes in me will never die. Do you believe this?'" (John 11:25–26).

Heaven is indubitable: "Do not let your hearts be troubled. Trust in God; trust also in me. In my Father's house are many rooms; if it were not so, I would have told you. I am going there to prepare a place for you. And if I go and prepare a place for you, I will come back and take you to be with me that you also may be where I am" (John 14:1–3).

What Heaven Is Not:

Heaven has no tears. There will be no more sadness! I don't know about you, but that promise is a thrill to my heart. To instantaneously be at continual peace with no cause for sadness is a blessed thought (Rev. 21:4).

Heaven does not have day and night sequences. Being eternal, time will not be measured by the 24-hour time periods that we know on this earth. Eternity is timeless. Forever literally means "forever." The word itself boggles the human mind. There will be no time barriers nor need for the sun or the moon since there is no day and night (Rev. 21:23–25).

Heaven will not have churches. The Bible tells us that the temple was a symbol of the presence of God. Since God himself is present in heaven, there is no need of a temple there (Rev. 21:3). The ultimate community of international believers from every nation and race will worship God together forever in perfect harmony (Rev. 19:1).

Heaven does not have drudgery. We will serve and work in heaven, but the agony and dread of labor will be gone (Rev. 14:13; 22:3). One of the results of sin was the curse of toil and working. In heaven we will enjoy our work. The curse will be gone.

Heaven has no death. Since death means sadness and separation, there is no death in heaven. We will live forever with God and others who die in Christ (Rev. 20:14; 22:3). Sin will be no more; thus death, sin's result, will also be gone forever.

Homeless No More

What awesome truths! Heaven is the wonderful, eternal home of every believer. Unending joy awaits us; separated from earth's impurities and imperfections. Heaven is a place of worship, praise, and service rendered unto our Lord . . . FOREVER!!!

One of the most poignant truths in life is that we all start out homeless. Perhaps I never really understood that statement until I met Lori Ann, a young woman in her late

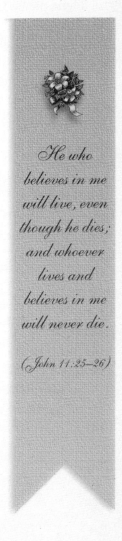

He who believes in me will live, even though he dies; and whoever lives and believes in me will never die.

(John 11:25–26)

teens. She lived at the shelter for single moms where our Mindy worked last year.

Oh sure, I had seen people on the highway with signs that read, "Help the homeless." Unmoved by their sad faces and silent pleas, I've always driven swiftly by. *Then* I had a name put to one of those faces. When Mindy introduced me to Lori Ann and her precious little baby, Kimberly, that all changed.

Lori Ann made a commitment to Christ and discovered the purpose and joy that He brings. She made room in her life for church, Bible study, and countless opportunities for increasing in knowledge of God and His Word.

I will never forget the night I drove her back to the shelter after a meeting. Instead of complaining about where she was to pillow her head that night, Lori Ann's focus was on the truths she had begun to discover. "I'm no longer homeless!" was her exclamation.

Rather than focusing on the status quo or what she *did not have,* Lori Ann delighted in *what she knew she did have.* Here was a girl who had very little of what this world has to offer. What made a permanent difference in her life each and every day was her new-found hope in Christ. She would never be homeless again — her home awaits her in heaven!

God's love for His people is not determined by the circumstances of our lives. His love is steadfast. Our marital status, career, finances . . . all might fluctuate or break apart. In spite of that, however, we can give thanks for His love toward us. It makes a tremendous difference in how we all approach life.

One of the mansions being prepared in heaven now bears Lori Ann's name and eternal address. Someday, Jesus will welcome her home. He will be her personal guide through each spacious room. No more pressures. No fear of personal failure. No energy, water, financial, or personal crisis there. No wonder she can hardly wait! Me, too! I'm looking forward to that glorious day!

Welcome Home, My Child!

Jesus hasn't forgotten about you! No matter what state your home is in right now, He holds you close to His heart. At this writing, the entire family room in our house is in total disarray due to water leakage. Our electricity went off for hours stopping our sump pump. Groan. Just five minutes ago I groped my way amid the maze of furniture — all shoved to the room's middle allowing carpet along the walls to dry out.

No matter what state your home is in right now, Jesus holds you close to His heart.

I made my way through the twists and turns and narrow places; thinking of a zillion trails I would have rather trekked along today. It's a pilgrimage I've encountered "far too many times in nine years living in this house," I heard myself grumbling aloud. "Why couldn't we have moved someplace where this didn't happen? Somewhere we didn't have to spend our free time repairing, rearranging, mopping."

You and I encounter differing struggles. We all take different roads home, each facing our own variety of twists and turns in the road. Do you despair, as I often do, in the journey? Remember, just like God said He would be, He's in control. He is always up to something in each of our lives. We need only to wait and watch His plan unfold. He is even now preparing a new, wonderful home for each of us, His children. "Do not let your hearts be troubled . . . in my Father's house are many rooms. . . . I am going there to prepare a place for you" (John 14).

Soon, very soon perhaps, the trumpet *will* sound. The Lord himself will descend from heaven with a shout. The dead in Christ will rise first; then we who are alive shall be caught up with them in the clouds to meet the Lord in the air. And so shall we ever be with the Lord!

There is no greater comfort to come home to . . . than knowing our final destination is a glorious home, where we will live forever with the great Comforter!

No sagging body, no cellulite, no weariness nor impending stress. This earthly body will be traded for a brand new, healthy one. Wars, bombings of public buildings, and shootings in schools will be things of the past. We will rest happily in eternal glory cradled in the arms of Jesus' sweet embrace.

Even if the cement is not yet dry on the first brick of your earthly house, don't look down. Look up toward the real estate you hold on high. With open arms, we will be welcomed to a place of comfort beyond the reaches of our imagination. He doesn't care what we look like, where we've been, or who we are. God just cares that we come. He will provide the home and all the comfort our hearts could ever desire.

I can't wait!

You Get by Giving

Have you ever wanted to pass along some hope to a friend, but are still wondering where to go to get a dose for yourself first? A few years ago I learned a secret that has brought a lot of hope, comfort, and joy. Give away the very thing you need the most. Sounds like a paradox, doesn't it? But, it's surprisingly the only sure road to real hope-filled living.

When you are low on funds, give some money (even a small amount) to someone who needs it more. If your four children under six are preventing you from having time alone, then try offering another young mother an afternoon or two a week to care for her children. You'll be thrilled when she reciprocates. Voila! There's your afternoon for time to yourself!

While you're searching for some hope for yourself, become a hope-giver to someone else. We are not to give to get, but it simply works that way following the principle of sowing and reaping. I find that when I give away *something that is precious to me,* to *someone who is precious to me,* I end up receiving much more than I have given!

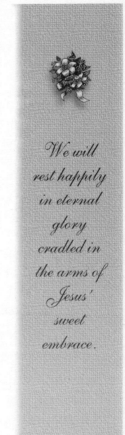

You can start with something as simple as a note or letter of hope to a friend, "I don't know how you feel, I can't really put myself in your situation, but I do know what makes me feel better. . . ." Then proceed to tell a story of a time when you felt hopeless and how you got through it. Guess who will be blessed? By giving a gift of hope, you will be blessed as much as your friend!

Look for the hope all around you. It's there! If you are willing to *look,* you will find bright spots in even the darkest day. *But, you have to LOOK!* Hope is everywhere! And you can't out-give God!

Go looking for hope today. It may be your only chance — you have to *at least try!*

We will rest happily in eternal glory cradled in the arms of Jesus' sweet embrace.

All That Glitters Is Not "Hope"

One day not so long ago, when I was having to *look hard* to find hope, a note came across my desk that made me smile. Along with the smile came laughter and hope. Just when I thought I was the only one in the world who had done irreversible, stupid things, I realized I am not alone. Other women do crazy things, too. Read on. I hope the same smile that came to my face reaches you.

In Melbourne, one of the radio stations paid money ($100-500) for people to tell their most embarrassing stories. This one netted the $500. The winner wrote:

I was due later that week for an appointment with the gynecologist when early one morning I received a call from his office that I had been rescheduled for that morning at 9:30 a.m. I had only just packed everyone off to work and school and it was around 8:45 a.m.

The trip to his office usually took about 35 minutes so I didn't have any time to spare. As most women do, I'm sure, I like to take a little extra effort over hygiene when making such visits, but this time I wasn't going to be able to make the full effort.

So I rushed upstairs, threw off my dressing gown, wet the washcloth and gave myself a wash in "that area" in front of the sink, taking extra care to make sure that I was presentable. I threw the washcloth in the clothes basket, donned some clothes, hopped in the car and raced to my appointment.

I was in the waiting room only a few minutes when he called me in. Knowing the procedure, as I am sure you all do, I hopped up on the table, looked over at the other side of the room and pretended I was in Hawaii or some other place a million miles away from here. I was a little surprised when he said: "My . . . we have taken a little extra effort this morning, haven't we?" But, I didn't respond. With the appointment over, I heaved a sigh of relief and went home.

The rest of the day went normal — some shopping, cleaning, and the evening meal, etc. At 8:30 p.m. that evening my 18-year-old daughter was fixing to go to a school dance, when she called down from the bathroom, "Mom, where's my washcloth?" I called back for her to get another from the cabinet.

She called back, "No, I need the one that was here by the sink, it had all my glitter and sparkles in it."

You see, just about the time you think you're the only one who has ever been humiliated, or hurt, or embarrassed beyond belief . . . think of this *sparkling* woman. What place in your heart do you need to fill with hope today? Fill in the blank: _____. Neither money, possessions, power, education, nor careers can provide the hope you're searching for. Don't waste your time trying to find hope in *things*. Call out to God's love. Nothing else satisfies. When you cry out to Him, "Help," He answers, "I'm already here!"

No one need be hopeless. No one!

Turn Up the Heat

Creating an atmosphere of hope in your home can be likened to regulating your thermostat to set a comfortable temperature inside your house. *Someone* has to punch in the numbers to set a proper degree. Unchecked, you will freeze in the winter and scorch in the summer. Similarly, our homes' emotional climate needs to be properly set. It is then, and only then, that home becomes a restful place where spirits are renewed in a comfortable ambiance.

Just as quickly as the seasons change, so can my home's climate. Left unchecked, our home can go from serene calm to swelling chaos in no time! Just this morning my office began to feel arctic-cold. After putting on socks and a heavy sweater, I finally got smart and turned up the thermostat. Duh! Soon I heard the furnace kicking on to warm things up. Similarly, *I* can become my

home's thermostat! When things get ice-cold, instead of giving everyone the cold shoulder, I can turn up the heat! I can be the one who regulates "climate" in my home by setting an atmosphere that renews the spirit physically, spiritually, and emotionally. We all can!

This is especially important on those days when icy winds of hopelessness are blowing strong — frosty gusts. You know those days. You're given the cold shoulder. Emotional icicles hang from the ceiling in every room. Someone needs to turn up the heat. *You* be the one! Infuse your home with HOPE — nothing warms the heart better.

Hope Makes a Difference

HOPE looks for the good in people instead of harping on the worst in them.

HOPE opens doors where despair closes them.

HOPE discovers what can be done instead of grumbling about what cannot be done.

HOPE draws its power from a deep trust in God and the basic goodness of mankind.

HOPE "lights a candle" instead of "cursing the darkness."

HOPE regards problems, small or large, as opportunities.

HOPE cherishes no illusions, nor does it yield to cynicism.

Anonymous

Take Hope — You Are Not Alone!

Nothing can turn a mom to the Lord quite so desperately as seeing her child in pain. I remember standing in the emergency room of a hospital biting the sides of my cheeks until they were shredded as I watched doctors stitching Mindy's bleeding ankle. She was only three years old at the time and *I felt responsible.* Mindy had been riding on the fender of my bicycle and I turned a corner too sharply into loose gravel. I blamed myself for her pain. After all, I *caused* the accident, didn't I?

Don't waste your time trying to find hope in things. Call out to God's love.

But that was small compared to the ripping apart of my heart that I experienced years later when Mindy was in trouble and a thousand miles away at college. I found myself stuck in a dark tunnel of despair. Couldn't see even a ray of light at the end. Hopeless. Broken dreams make us feel that way.

Right now you may be hurting from a broken dream. Hopeless. You haven't even been stitched up yet. In fact, your whole life may seem like an emergency room. Desperately, you want things to change! But, don't know how they can . . . or if they ever will. *It won't last forever!* Whatever you're going through, you can have hope knowing that "this too, shall pass."

You are not facing your future alone.

This following poem by my Mindy says it all so well. She will forever have my inexhaustible thanks to her for surprising me with such a glorious gift at last year's mother-daughter banquet. There was not a dry eye in the auditorium when she finished at the grand piano singing and playing these words to me before four hundred women. May it give you reason to hope, as it has to me and so many.

"I AM NOT ALONE"

Day by day . . .
They've gone so fast
And now I stand here grown.
My world once small
But times have past
And now, I'm on my own.
You've been there with me,
Held my hand tightly.
When I would fall, you'd pick me up.
Then taught me how to stand.
Today I know you differently
Than I've ever known before.
Though you're not always right next to me
I realize more and more
That I am not alone.

When I am weak and *cannot* stand
Now, you can't pick me up.
You've left me to One who can,
That has to be enough.
And when my hand is just too far
You can't hold on — as in the past.
Though it may bring tears
You loosen your loving grasp
And you let me go
Into the arms that can bring me safely home.
There I find you on your knees
And I know . . .
That I am not alone.

Through all my years
You've stood beside me
You walked along life's road.
And then I would often wander
You'd carried my massive load.
But, today my load's too heavy
For even the both of us to bear.
Now, He's waiting to carry me
Because He heard your prayer.
We've created a bond between us
Stronger than the winds that blow.
Though time and miles are against us
This one thing I'll always know —
That I am not alone.
      — by Mindy Elaine Hoffman

Instant in Every Season

I was feeling rather smug after having taken advantage of a warm winter day to take down my outdoor holiday decorations. Up and down our block, many of my neighbors had done the same. All but one. I couldn't help noticing the Christmas grapevine wreath still hanging at the top of the garage door of a neighbor-hood friend's house. Every time I rounded the corner it's message continued to wish passersby a Merry Christmas. For weeks! *She probably is busy and the Iowa winter now is too rough to be climbing up a ladder,* I thought.

Well into February, with the street covered with snow, I looked up to catch a glimpse of something new attached to the wreath. I practically slid through the icy intersection straining to see what it was that was different about my friend's wreath. It was a bright red heart wishing all "Happy Valentines' Day!"

A few weeks later, the wreath was outlined with green shamrocks throughout March. Two weeks before Easter, a pretty yellow ribbon and a darling floppy-eared bunny appeared and stayed throughout April. The merry month of May came . . . and so did little wooden tulips announcing that spring had finally arrived.

With the warmer weather, I stopped my car one afternoon when I saw Debbie outside her home. I told her how much I'd enjoyed the "changing of the wreath" for the past few months. Even though she and I had not gotten to chat all winter, I told Debbie that I felt as though we had! Her wreath was an almost daily reminder to me of the joy that Debbie is to all she meets. "We have so much to celebrate, I just thought we would celebrate all year long!" she told me.

And celebrate she does! Just being in her presence was a blessing and reminded me that every day, *I can find something to celebrate!* The Lord was using Debbie's wreath as a visual object lesson to minister her life message . . . even when we weren't getting together in person, I was still being blessed by a dear friend who had reason to celebrate all year long.

Similarly, Moses instructed the Israelites to keep annual seasonal celebrations and hang "memorials before their eyes" (Exod. 13:9) so that their families would not forget that the Lord had brought them out of Egypt. They were to celebrate the Passover annually and make certain their children knew why.

Keeping a house is fairly easy; a house is visible. A home is not so visible; thus, keeping a *home* is more difficult. God specifically calls upon women to be the "keepers at home" (Titus 2 :5). One of the ways we can do that is to celebrate what blessings we're enjoying in our lives. Yes, to even hang them on the "doorposts of our homes." May the Lord help us all to hang a wreath on the doorpost of our hearts, reminding even ourselves of the many blessings we have to celebrate.

And give Him the glory, great things He hath done!

Believe it or not, by June a red, white, and blue flag appeared and continued on the wreath through July. And in August . . . month after month Debbie's message of cheer rang out!

> Praise the Lord,
>   Praise the Lord,
> Let the earth hear His voice.
>   Praise the Lord,
> Praise the Lord,
>   Let the people rejoice.
> Oh, come to the Father
>   Through Jesus the Son
> And give Him the glory,
>   Great things He hath done!
>   — Fanny Crosby

By the Book!

I am no mathematical genius. Believe me, that's putting it mildly. (Take a peek at my checkbook!) When I was in high school, I studied math that was taught during the sixties. After nearly driving numerous teachers to the point of exasperation, I finally made it through algebra and geometry. Much of what I learned is now extinct due to computers and calculators. Unfortunately, the excuse "*I'll never use this!*" never got me out of doing the work while in school. I memorized abhorrent figures, graphs, and measurements that simply no longer exist. Even while assisting my daughters with their homework ten years ago, I was made to see how antiquated my math skills had become.

How thankful I am to know there is one factual equation that makes sense to me. Its validity can never become obsolete because it comes from God's word. The passage is Philippians 4:6–7. No matter how you sum it up, you will arrive at the same answer every time! You won't find it to be a bewildering, rote-memorized mathematic procedure. Even the math-challenged like me can understand this base formula:

Prayer + Supplication + Thanksgiving = PEACE

God's Will for Us

Just to be tender, just to be true;
Just to be glad the whole day through.
Just to be merciful, just to be mild;
Just to be trustful as a child.
Just to be gentle and kind and sweet,
Just to be helpful with willing feet.
Just to be cheery when things go wrong,
Just to drive sadness away with a song.
Whether the hour is dark or bright,
Just to be loyal to God and right.
Just to believe that God knows best,
Just in His promise ever to rest;
Just to let love be our daily key,
This is God's will, for you and me.

Anonymous

To the Book

How well I remember our daughter Missy's frustration when a math assignment consisted not only of the correct answer to a problem, but showing the *proof*, as well. "After all," Mr. Whitehouse would exhort the sixth graders, "you don't want to grow up to be a french-fry shoveler all your life!" It was those "proofs" that got to Missy! She would struggle at the kitchen table many a late evening working on draft after draft. And, mind you, Missy was *not exactly her usual perky self* during these intense sessions. "I don't know how I got the answer, *it just works!*" As I recall, the rest of the family was inclined to slip as far away as we all could to escape the frustrating ordeal. By the time her answers began to make sense, Missy would often have filled a wastebasket with wadded papers and endless columns of numerals.

When Missy got stuck on a problem that was beyond both of our reasoning, I'd wearily end my tutorial session with a frustrated "Just go look in the book!" (Promptly I'd then exit the room in delirium.) Now, why didn't we think of that before! It never failed. Later in the evening, Missy would calmly emerge with relief written all over her face and join the family in whatever we were doing.

And the peace of God, which transcends all understanding, will guard your hearts and your minds in Christ Jesus.

(Phil. 4:7)

Sound familiar? Our daily lives are often as complicated as a math problem. Things just don't add up. I'm so glad the formula for peace is not as difficult, nor does it take so long to find the "proof." That is, IF WE GO TO THE BOOK. We all have doubts, frustrations, and questions that just don't seem to add up . . . no matter how we align the variables. God's peace for us comes to our hearts when we trust in *His* plan for our lives. Not in our own. Life's equation never comes to the right answer when we manipulate the equation to get our own way.

"Be still and know that I am God" (Ps. 46:10) means "Relax, let God figure it out." In times of confusion when we find it difficult to "prove" what's going on — God is still God. He truly knows what is best. His ways are not our ways. I shudder to think how things would have turned out if I had my way in many circumstances of my life. In His loving kindness, God will provide the peace, if we follow the formula.

You don't have to know how to add, subtract, multiply, or divide! In Philippians the formula is clear, concise, and constant. It transcends all natural explanations. We may not know *how* it works . . . *"it just works!" By the Book.*

Some Things Worth Keeping

Rather than having "Aha!" experiences, more often God lets us know His truths in a new and personal way through events in our everyday lives. Such was my reward while attempting to clean the garage last spring. I desired a clean garage, but I didn't want to give up any "stuff." And, girlfriend, we had *lots of stuff!*

Standing at the door measuring from every angle, I realized what Rob had said earlier that morning was right. "No way, no how, are two cars going to fit into our garage next winter unless we get rid of a lot of this stuff!" Rob and I usually feel like we make a pretty good pair. I guess, like a well-fitting pair of shoes, we're a good fit. We walk in stride. But, early in this particular day I knew that I was the one out of step.

Have you ever tried to walk in a pair of high heels when one heel was broken off? Before long, the limping causes you to feel miserable. Rob says that he was attracted to me in college because of my gregarious personality. Little did he know at the time, however, was that sanguines are sentimental pack rats. We want to hold on to everything! Eliminating some of our 26 years of family memories was unthinkable to me! I had tried unsuccessfully for years to part with "treasures" such as the huge stuffed teddy bear that Missy won on the church bus at age five.

As I surveyed the area before attempting the formidable task at hand, I was plagued by a question I've asked myself more than once during the past 26 years. "Why is it that people tend to seek out and marry our opposite?" Sociologists answer that it is universal: We marry someone who has the characteristics we lack. God explains: "the two shall become one flesh" (Gen. 2:24).

In the midst of all my rearranging, streamlining, sorting, and trashing, God began to reveal one of Rob's great strengths. Acknowledging Rob's sense of order as one of his best inborn traits, I saw where I had allowed it to become a source of contention, rather than blessing. What if we'd both hung on to every sentimental piece of paper or stuffed animal for all these years? No U-Haul truck made would have been able to help haul all the "stuff" out.

And like someone once pointed out: *"Even the best things in life are still just things."*

The two shall become one flesh.

(Gen. 2:24)

Why then do couples let the very "opposites" that first drew us to one another later become the very sources of painful friction and irritation? With me, I know it's because I want to be right. *My way is best,* I say to myself. And there are times that when I don't get my way, I let Rob have it with both barrels.

I spent all morning cleaning out the clutter in our garage. I made such a scene, with sorting boxes all up and down our long driveway, a couple of people stopped in their cars to ask if I was having a garage sale. (I probably should have!)

Some items posed a difficult choice — some were tossed; some stayed. More importantly, I chose to clean some attitudes toward Rob that I'd allow to clutter my heart, too. To fulfill an ongoing process of becoming *one,* I needed to take a fresh look at Rob's strengths. I had to admit that our opposites actually add to our joys and togetherness as a couple. It was only a matter of time before I saw the power of that accepting attitude do its work.

It was later that month when Rob and I took a fall foliage trip through eastern Iowa. We had been driving on the highway only a short time when we came within seconds of being part of a serious car accident. Were it not that we were spared by what I believe were God's angels, we would have been hit head-on. Shaken, we stopped by the side of the road to check on those injured and to quiet our nerves.

How thankful I was to have had a fresh reminder in my garage weeks earlier of how special Rob is. I could have lost him without giving him the appreciation he deserves. I simply chose to agree with God that he is an instrument through which God's love becomes evident to me. It's futile when we try to run our homes without God. We run into such big trouble when we do. Try cleaning out some of the "stuff" cluttering your heart today, won't you?

(Added note: Yes, Missy's prized bear made the "cut" . . . one more time!)

PERSONAL OR GROUP STUDY GUIDE • WEEK 6

1. What is the most important impression of heaven that these verses leave upon you?

1 Cor. 2:9	Rev. 21:4	1 Thess. 4:17
John 11:25–26	John 14:1–3	

2. Are there any similarities that you see between a "keeper of home" and a "keeper of a heart"? Read Matthew 11:28,30; Titus 2:5; and Luke 10:38–42.

3. If you were attempting the formidable task of fitting another car in your garage, what would you toss out in order to make room? In your heart, are there "things" that can be set aside in order to unclutter your life so you might be able to make a greater eternal difference in the lives of others?

4. Hope lets one "see light at the end of the tunnel." What is the formula that Phil. 4:6–7 gives us to find peace while on this earth?

_____ & _____ & _____ = PEACE

5. We cannot go to Jesus face-to-face with our problems, so how can we approach Him? Read Jeremiah 33:3; John 16:24; Philippians 4:6; and 2 Chronicles 7:14–15.

6. Prayer is asking our loving Heavenly Father, "What would You have me to do?" He longs to hear from His children off and on all day long. Prayer is the only way we can be "anxious for nothing." Isaiah 40:31 tells us how we will not faint. Read that passage right alongside Psalm 57:1 and Psalm 34:6.

PRAYER PARAGRAPH
Finish writing this prayer paragraph to honor God in all we do: Precious Lord, put a longing in my heart for my heavenly home, that I might long for more than this present world. I pray I might be found faithful in all areas including _____
_____
_____

Lovingly,
Your Daughter

Come Home to Harmony

"Catch-up" in the Kitchen

The kitchen is often called the "heart of the home." Ours certainly is. My family's physical bodies are nourished there. We gather round the kitchen table to regroup and re-fresh. Preparing meals and eating together easily opens the doors for interaction. Many of the most satisfying moments with family and friends have been spent sharing a meal and sweet conversation together.

My kitchen seems to be the room, above all other rooms in our house, that is filled with love and warmth. Comfort reigns. Some of my most treasured conversations with Rob have taken place as we reconnect at the table after a busy day. After-school or midnight snacks provided the perfect occasions in a casual setting to teach Missy and Mindy in their younger years, "line upon line, precept upon precept."

We probably spend more time in our kitchen "funning" and "fellowshiping" than we do eating. Lingering over a cup of coffee, reading the Sunday paper, finishing homework projects . . . our kitchen is the room that adapts to these many uses. Truly, the real expression of our day-to-day living goes on in our kitchen. In fact, the back door entrance to our home opens right into the kitchen, making it a focal point and hub of our family life.

While we were renovating our house, we addressed the kitchen first because of its prominence. The transformation began to come together when I tried to recall what it is about my favorite restaurant that gives me such pleasure. We then set out to recreate that same ambiance in our own kitchen/dining area. We wanted to include plenty of natural light, comfortable seating, and calming colors. It would be uncluttered, useful, yet with decorative touches of charm and character — altogether fashioned in just the right design and atmosphere we had envisioned.

It gives me great pleasure to know that our kitchen feeds not only bodies, but also replenishes the souls of those who enter. That is my prayer. I desire that all who enter might feel loved and fed emotionally — right down to their soul. Because I personally pass through our kitchen many times a day, I enjoy doing the small gestures that mean so much in keeping the atmosphere conducive to nourishment of the soul.

The best houses have an abundance of heart! That's what instills the spirit of good emotional health. Unpretentious and homey touches can have a deep emotional effect on us. God has created us to respond in our brains to what we see and smell. Fragrant candles, fresh flowers (go ahead, spring for them as you check out the next time at the grocery!), a bowl of sunny lemons to cheer . . . all ideas right at your fingertips! In a kitchen bustling with activity, these small touches of comfort can have an uplifting effect on every member of the family. It's a shame to use them only for company or holidays.

Labors of Love

No matter how modern or conveniently efficient your kitchen is, it is there that you carry out the task of loving others . . . not just cooking for others. If you are a mom, you are teaching many domestic lessons by sheer example. One of the essential ingredients for any home manager is to remember: Good, healthy eating patterns will last the family for a lifetime and pleasurable mealtimes are memories held forever. It is in this way that our grown children never fully leave home. My adult daughters both have homes of their own now but still tell me how certain aromas invoke recollections and warm feelings of home.

Bread dough rising, then baking . . . cinnamon . . . fresh coffee (umm, raspberry chocolate) . . . garlic in homemade spaghetti sauce . . . these are all kitchen scents that trigger my daughters to call long distance. Whatever the season, our kitchen has been a comforting spirit in each of our souls through everyday life. Edith Schaeffer says it well: "The cook in the home has the opportunity to be doing something very real in the area of making good human relationships." The older I get, the more I agree!

Most folks, whether company or family, enter our home through the kitchen door. I see each person who enters my home as someone special. To remind me and them of this, I love to look at my kitchen as a "comfort station." Making a kitchen into a place to lovingly serve helps combat having an attitude of dreaded drudgery. "Better a dry crust with peace and quiet than a house full of feasting, with strife" (Prov. 17:1). You'll be inspired to spend more time there if you perform even the smallest task as "unto the Lord" (Col. 3:23).

Ruth Bell Graham had a sign posted for years above her kitchen sink that read:

Ministry performed here three times a day.

Pouring Cups of Love

I try to remember the above admonition when I feel like dishes are a meaningless drudgery. The choice is yours and mine. We can either choose to resent or to rejoice as we nourish others. Even if the recipients fail to appreciate a sweet attitude, God sees it. It is better to serve a meager meal lovingly, than a banquet where bickering and strife abound (see Prov. 15:17). God always puts it all in perspective, doesn't He? It's not the menu that matters. How it is served and with what *attitude* is what's important!

It's those small acts of care that satisfy my husband more than the "biggies." After a stressful day I love to slip into the kitchen and pour two glasses of Rob's favorite tea. Then maybe I'll place two of his favorite chocolate cookies on a pretty napkin or dish. Pausing to serve my husband in the midst of life's busyness does as much good for me as it does Rob. It sits us still. Quiets our souls. It lets someone dear to me know he is loved and cared for. Those moments of tranquillity uplift us both.

Are there unhealthy relationships in your home that you need to care for? How about dusting off a pretty tray and serving your loved one his or her favorite beverage and sweet treat? Take time to relax and converse together. It takes little effort, but to your family it says they are loved. They will remember the sweet communication and times shared for years. I once heard that the word "love" could be spelled

Better a dry crust with peace and quiet than a house full of feasting, with strife.

(Prov. 17:1)

"t-i-m-e." Spending time one with another is a gift that says "You are loved."

Lovin' in the Oven

A woman in one of my conferences this year wrote me that she "has begun to view her kitchen as the center of her ministry." She used to drag herself into the kitchen each morning and view the room as "functional, yet just a place to perform necessary routines." With two small children constantly vying for her attention, it was difficult for Dorothy to find quiet ways to comfort her husband. She longed to restore the closeness she and Stan had once shared in their marriage.

A month or so after the women's conference a letter arrived at my home. I tore it open and began to read eagerly.

"Dear Sharon . . . dear, *dear* Sharon . . . my *dear, dear, dear!*"

Dorothy had stocked her kitchen with love, not just canned goods! And what a spice it was bringing to her marriage! Her recipe was simple. Instead of always putting the children first and never taking time for Stan, she had begun to work hard on having a sweet spirit in her home. Stan loved sweets on the table, but had told her "he'd rather have a sweet wife than sweets for desert any day!"

Determined to make their home a place of comfort, Dorothy added attractive touches to her kitchen. Simple

things like flowers on the table and a candle's glow on the counter did wonders for her own attitude toward this room. She moved a small radio and began to play soothing, inspirational music to set a calm spirit in her own heart. Little note cards with quotes of encouragement and Scripture were placed on the refrigerator and other key areas.

The very first evening after *remodeling* her kitchen, Dorothy came home from work drained. You might know, so did Stan. Still, determined to use her kitchen for ministering to her family, Dorothy prepared a simple, yet delicious dinner. She listened to Stan talking about his day without interruption and preoccupation. He talked and talked. She said he had never talked so much!

"If it hadn't been for the children," she said, "I think he would have thrown me down right there on the kitchen floor! Instead, we put the kids to bed very early!" A change of attitude toward your kitchen changes all sorts of things! Maybe even your love life!

Healthy, Happy, and Hospitable Kitchens

While the primary function of the kitchen is eating, there is no other room in the house where so much goes on that involves the whole family at one time. Keep the following three qualities in mind to make your kitchen *the* place to be.

Healthy — Clean Up Our Act!

Delicious, nutritious meals begin with knowledge of the nutrients that our bodies need and the understanding of good nutrition. Six nutrients that assist in the regulation of body processes have been listed as: carbohydrates, fats, protein, vitamins, minerals, and water. Properly balancing a diet of the foods that

Do what you can with what you have where you are.

Theodore Roosevelt (1858–1919)

contain these nutrients will result in optimum health for your body and mind.

Much work has been done to determine requirements for various age groups and in circumstances of individual needs. I have found that my cooking and my family's eating habits have changed drastically over the last ten years. With numerous health-conscious books and magazines readily available, I am constantly reading more about the importance of nutrition (age, you say?).

Good eating as a lifestyle helps you keep up with an active lifestyle, plus insures defenses against aging. Great beauty tip! I can tell when I have eaten healthy and when I have not. It really shows after I eat junk all weekend or while traveling. Puffiness, darkness under my eyes, weariness . . . just an overall droopy look. When I eat and drink healthy, I look like it! Getting those eight glasses of water a day makes a big difference alone!

Let children help with food preparation. It makes eating it a lot more fun and teaches good nutrition and cleanliness. You will also find your children more apt to try new foods if they help to prepare them.

Counting fat grams is not all there is to eating healthy. We've all been down the low-fat trail many times . . . and back again. The secret to looking good and living long is to clean up your act . . . your eating act, that is. Clean out all that grease! Low-fat eating used to be low on flavor, too. Today, supermarkets offer such a wide array of fresh produce and aisles full of satisfying, reduced-fat items that make it much easier on the budget and eating habits. This is great news for us snack-a-holics!

Do your body a favor. Learn all you can about healthy foods and adjust old family favorite recipes to new low-fat substitutes. It won't take long before your taste buds start to tingle as you desire a taste for fattier foods. Resist it! As you modify your lifestyle from high in fat to high in health, the rewards are well worth it! You won't *want* to turn back. YOU *CAN* LOOSE THE FAT, BUT KEEP THE FLAVOR! I like to use lemon, herbs, and spices to liven up less flavorful foods instead of adding fats or oils.

"If you replace fat with other more filling, nutrient-dense foods, you can actually lose pounds while eating more," says Annette Natow, R.D., Ph.D., of Nutrition Consultants in Valley Stream, New York. Cheese is one of the most common fat boosters in a woman's diet. Minimize it and choose light-colored varieties like mozzarella, Swiss, and ricotta.

A change of attitude toward your kitchen changes all sorts of things!

Go for the Green

Brans and grains are not the only source of health. Fresh fruits and seasonal vegetables can add a lot to your decor on the table or counter. I enjoy having them visible. It is not only pleasing to the eye but to the taste as a quick, pick-up snack, as well. It's better than reaching for a chocolate bar or six Oreos!

The bottom line: if health is among your goals for your family, a nutrition-packed kitchen is just the beginning of healthy a lifestyle. Judy Dodd, R.D., former president of the American Dietetic Association and a nutrition adviser says, "There are no *bad foods, only bad eating habits*, which are easy to change if you take things one step at a time."

Happy — Take Time to Smell the Baking

Make your kitchen a room that is so inviting that family and friends (and you!) will want to linger in its welcoming warmth. Your day begins in the kitchen, so start it with items that surround you with joy. If you have to, revolutionize your kitchen with touches that boost your personal happiness. I guess it all comes down to the fact that you can't love others unless you first love yourself. And that would make a great title for a country-western song!

Simplicity Is the Key

Set aside some of those appliances cluttering the countertops. Store them away in low cabinets. Hang a pretty basket or two — or ten. In just five minutes you can "de-junk" your kitchen every day. I know. I have to daily since we enter and drop, enter and drop, enter and . . . well, you get the idea. Your room will look more spacious and you will be more relaxed while working in a less cluttered area.

Take time in your kitchen to smell the roses — and the baking! I am a breadmaker and my family loves to come home to the oven's fragrance of bread baking. Nothing conjures up the feeling of home's coziness and comfort more than warm bread. Maybe you are not a bread maker. Some women will never be. That's fine. When you do want the wonderful scent, freezer loaves are a simple solution and just as pleasurable as homemade.

Simmering Secrets

Certainly you will find your own sweet smells to fill your kitchen — mouth-watering scents like soup simmering and desserts slipped in the oven during the meal to be served warm. When on days, like recently, there is no time for home cooking, I love to drop a scented wax tart into a small potpourri pot. They come in kitchen fragrances like cinnamon spice, vanilla, pumpkin, cranberry, apple . . . yum, and they last for days. At least that way I have the homey smells coming forth from my kitchen even if there is nothin' in the oven.

Hey, these days, I go by the Hoffman Code of Home Cooking: "If you so much as *buy* a meal within five miles of your home . . . you can call it "homemade!"

Let Your Little Light Shine

Ask yourself if you have a joyful atmosphere in your kitchen. If we want our families to express happy hearts, it has to begin with us. It must be *caught,* not just taught. What a shame that it has become a natural part of many mealtimes to fall into a pattern of sarcasm, complaining, and a time to air frustrations. Everyone leaves the table feeling depressed, rather than with their spirits lifted.

Hold off on the negative concerns until after everyone has a chance to share uplifting conversation. Perhaps the most effective way to bring a relaxing, peaceful mode at mealtime is to make it a habit of inviting God to be present at every meal. By beginning mealtimes with a blessing and thankful prayer, you are helping to turn hearts in the direction of gratitude and peace. Pausing to gather together is a blessing in and of itself. Even a hurried rote-memory blessing is better than none. Our family long ago began the habit of stopping to hold hands, and asks the Lord's blessing on our food and those gathered at every meal.

You can't love others unless you first love yourself.

Let the sun shine in your kitchen with generous doses of the natural light shining through. Being a "morning person," I like the bright sunshine in the early morning. I've topped windows with a puffed valance, balloon, or swag for a soft effect. I make the most of the sun's rays in our kitchen by using a floral lace for a cottage look. The outdoor view and sun's rays brighten my outlook, is relaxing, and brings the outdoors inside.

Doctors who studied the effect of rooms with outdoor views have found patients less anxious, more energetic, and with higher doses of serotonin — which I understand is a mood-booster that we all could use plenty of! Let the sun shine in!

The way a home is lit will greatly affect its ambiance and comfort. If you are squinting to read the paper at the breakfast counter or to rinse dishes at the sink, you need to lighten up your room. Because the light from overhead fixtures tends to be harsh, I enjoy placing small lamps here and there on my counter tops and window sills. They help to define and add depth to the room.

Similarly, I often use the soft glow of tiny white twinkle lights . . . not just for the holidays. Leave them up in places all through your home all year around. Try twining them around ivy above your kitchen cabinets. What a welcoming sight when you walk in! Use them above windows through garland or to line a shelf. I have strung or tangled them among just about everything — from my fresh flower centerpiece to windows to the fixture above the kitchen table for a starry night effect.

Actual lighting fixtures and windows are not the only visual considerations when it comes to lighting your kitchen. YOU become a beacon of light! Don't just let your little self shine — *glow brightly* for all to see!

Hospitality — A Lost Art?

When I am a guest in someone else's home, what I notice most is not what food is served or if their coffee table is dusted or how many pillows are on their sofa. What I *do* remember is genuine kindness, an affirming hug, and a Christ-like joyful spirit that permeates the home.

Having company at your house in the near future? I will be. My kitchen will be a flurry of activity. As hosts, we need to remember the special touches that will help guests feel like family. Your warmth, smile, and welcoming ways will draw others to you and to your faith as you use the gift of hospitality. That's the goal. Not showing off materialistic possessions, but carrying out the admonition of loving and serving others.

In the process of pouring our lives into others our own cup begins to overflow.

In the whirlwind of your life, is hospitality almost a lost art? Let's bring it back! Inviting someone into your home says, "You are important to me and I love you." It can be as simple as a glass of iced tea on the patio or as lavish as a sit-down four-course dinner.

We don't even know the meaning of *that* term at our house, but I have made a habit of using Sunday dinners as opportunities of hospitality. It was those occasions that provided the hands-on training for my daughters to learn the joys of giving others the royal treatment. They both grew up knowing how to set a formal table, serve and refill drinks, and proper table manners by "reaching from the right and serving to the left!"

The key to hospitality is being sensitive to the needs of your guests and offering little extras that say "I care." In those ways we are truly living out 1 Peter 4:9–10 by practicing "hospitality one to another." We must not forget that some have "entertained angels unawares" that God sends our way to give us occasions to prove our compassion toward others.

Be sure not to reserve the spirit of hospitality for guests only. I really believe it should be an attitude in our homes every day; a sharing of our lives with those who know us best and need us the most — our families. The famous 31st chapter of Proverbs is a portrait of a hospitable woman. I want to be a godly woman like her. Hardworking. Hospitable. Industrious. Creative. Best of all, she delights in her role as a wife and mother and is a woman "who fears the Lord."

A woman such as she could put heart into any kitchen! Her reward is that her children arise and call her blessed; and her husband, also, he praises her greatly. Our motivation of loving certainly is not to *get,* but to *give.* Not to expect praise, but to please the Lord. In the process of pouring our lives into others, however, our own cup begins to overflow. I find I am filled and not as hungry for compliments or praise as I once was. Not that affirmation is not nice, but if I am pleasing God in proper motivation, I have deep satisfaction.

It's interesting that the word "hospitality" is wedged in my dictionary between "hospice," a place of shelter, and "hospital," a place of healing. Your dear home today can be that kind of retreat . . . a refuge where you are not seeking gratification, but a sanctuary where healing and shelter are offered to all who enter. Great satisfaction will naturally follow.

I have a dear prayer partner friend who has a special flair for this sort of thing with boundless energy. Her home is a constant source of entertaining. Liz loves to celebrate others' birthdays, afternoon teas, and holiday gatherings. She is not simply paying a social obligation, but is giving different people in our church an opportunity to relax and have a good time sharing their lives together as Christians. Liz has made a great contribution toward strengthening friendships in the body of Christ. I love going to her home. I come away feeling so loved!

Unexpected company coming? I seem to get that memo often lately and have learned a couple of quick cleaning tips that work. Run over the toilet, sink, counters, and faucets with a baby wipe. You're ready for visitors. In fact, having a friend over, even if just for coffee once a week, or a Bible study in your home inspires you (*forces me!*) to keep your home presentable. I keep my house presentable better if I have goals to shoot for.

The question is not what a man can scorn, or disparage, or find fault with, but what he can love and value and appreciate.

John Ruskin (1819–1900)

PERSONAL OR GROUP STUDY GUIDE • WEEK 7

1. When it is said that "a woman has her fingertips on the domestic pulse of her home," what is being referred to?

2. Read Proverbs 31:27. What are you doing to "watch over the affairs of your household"?

3. Evaluate your family's schedule. Are you able to eat at least one meal together a day? A week? Write out a realistic household schedule at the beginning of this week and plan accordingly. Is the time well spent or too spent?

4. Complete this sentence around the room: "Hospitality in my home in the last six months has included _____." (Share with your group or write out personally what steps you are presently [or will be] taking to contribute to this important ministry in your home.)

5. Sometimes we need an excuse to tidy up or fix up our home. Invite some company to your home this week. It may be a lavish dinner or simply a cup of coffee with a neighbor. Share with your group. It might be that you'd want to invite them over for some "cups of love." Let your little light shine!

6. Read Proverbs 15:17. Take time this week while you are alone; slowly walk through each room of your home as if you'd never toured it before. Prayer-walk as you go, thanking God for the privilege to live in the home God has entrusted to you. Pray for each person living there as you pause in their individual room.

PARAGRAPH PRAYER
Finish writing this paragraph prayer of tremendous gratefulness: Lord, I give you my ungrateful, grumbling spirit and in return I beg for_____

_____

_____

_____

Lovingly,
Your Daughter

Living in the Fast Food Lane!

You know how it is. From the moment the alarm rings in the morning, you are off and running. You make coffee, take a quick shower, get kids roused, dressed, and fed. Then it's get dressed and dash to work, spending eight hours or more on the job. After picking up your son at softball practice, dropping your daughter off at soccer, fixing dinner, and helping children with homework, you wind up doing paperwork before tomorrow's meeting. Whew! No wonder many women have the "5:30 Syndrome." We're frazzled, fussy, and faint! Suppertime follows, resembling a Chinese fire drill!

What motivates me is having a *PLAN.* I can work my plan and take great pride in my accomplishment. Without a plan, homemaking is just a daily grind. There is neither excitement nor fulfillment, much less a pride of performance on the job. It's just the same ol' same ol'. By paying attention to the following details in a simple plan any home can become a more healthy, pleasant place in which to be.

Following a plan is the secret in learning to do things the easiest, most pleasurable way possible! The number one reason I hear women say they do not like to cook is because they dislike the planning and shopping. One way to simplify menus for your family is to repeat the basic main entree every two weeks. Jot down five week-night supper meals and weekend meals that your family eats at home. Keep it simple. Then, before going to the grocery

Owe no man any thing, but to love one another: for he that loveth another hath fulfilled the law.

(Rom. 13:8 KJV)

store, you will know which week's list of items you need to take. The staples basically repeat every two weeks.

One main reason so many families drive through a fast-food is because they fail to plan. After a long, hectic day at the office or at home, who wants to drag in the front door and hear "What's for dinner?" One more decision sends us into overload! So, we end up serving unprepared, unappetizing meals with little nutritional value.

Planning will make your life much, much simpler. I spent too many years *not* doing "all things decently and in order" (1 Cor. 14:40). I am living proof that you can change! "A place for everything and everything in its place" the old adage goes. For the most part, yes, even as we begin the 21st century, duties of managing a home fall squarely on the shoulders of the woman of the house.

Women from countries literally all over the world have reported to me the awesome differences in their households when they began applying the "Twenty-Five Thousand Dollar Plan." I learned the principles of this plan as a newly married years ago in the seventies' "total woman" classes. They still work as well for me now as they did as a newly-wed.

It's the plan that management consultant Ivy Lee suggested to his CEO many years ago. He received $25,000 for suggesting this plan to the president of his company. The principles work when applied to household management as well. And believe me, it is worth every cent! No longer will you feel swamped with all you are juggling. You will be calmer, unrushed, and be able to *find the things you need when you need them!*

The Twenty-Five Thousand Dollar Plan

1. Every night write down the important things you need to accomplish the next day.

2. Number them in order as to importance (i.e., dental appointment, vacuum, etc.)

3. The next day, finish as much on your plan as is realistically possible. Do hardest tasks first.

4. When interruptions come, accept them, then go right on finishing each item.

Be realistic. Remember, our goal here is to *simplify*, not cause additional stress. The answer to disorderliness is not vacuuming four times a day or hourly running around the house with a feather duster. Fastidious "neatness neurotics" like that are killing themselves to keep up. (Then there are those of us who have had *Good Housekeeping* or *Better Homes and Gardens* threaten to cancel our magazine subscriptions!)

Tackling Time Enemies

Balance is the key. Too much structure can be just as frustrating as being haphazard. But, if you're like me, I find time is much too valuable a commodity to waste precious energy looking for misplaced items or having many unfinished projects lying around.

Plan. Do your countertops, tables, and desk stay cluttered? How about your closets and clothing? Are you readily able to put your hands on important papers and bills right away? Do you have a will and insurance documents in a

The best portions of a good man's life are his little, nameless, unremembered acts of kindness and love.

William Wordsworth (1770–1850)

protected place? Are you prompt to appointments and work? Is your attire matched, pressed, and shoes shined? Are you a time waster . . . phone talker . . . TV addict? Do you have to be in a hurry to get anywhere on time?

Ugh . . . I'm stepping on my own toes here. Instead of getting over-loaded, let's admit what our individual areas are that need attention. For two weeks faithfully use the Twenty-Five Thousand Dollar Plan and watch your calendar begin to be your friend rather than your worst enemy. Pace yourself.

Do not put on tomorrow's plan everything you should have been doing for the last six months. "Spring Cleaning" is not one point on your list. Too many targets will frustrate you. Remember, simplify . . . simplify . . . simplify!

Streamlining Your Work

Start today! Commitment is the significant ingredient that will motivate you to move from the pitfalls that trip you up and impede progress. Instead of procrastinating, begin today. *Plan. Prioritize. Progress. Pray.*

Prioritize. God puts high priority on organization and orderliness. Proverbs 24:30–34 describes the inefficient person as a "sluggard." "Decently and in order" is our goal!

The point is, when I did not organize my time, my chores ran me. I thought a schedule would be arbitrary and restrictive, but it turned out to be quite freeing. God is a God of order. He is able to use us and our talents best in an orderly fashion. If order is going to prevail in your home, at some point *you* are going to have to impose it.

Progress. Each woman's schedule must be tailored to her individual needs and the needs of her family. A new baby, children leaving home, extended illnesses, etc. obviously mean drastic alterations in the schedule. I find that at least once a year I must fine-tune my schedule. At the present, I have been using a "homemade" priority planner with dividers to mark each section. For years I frustrated myself with those pre-put-together notebooks, so I ended up making my own. In a small three-ring binder I made my own tabs for sections that applied to my personal calendar, "to-do's," and lifestyle. No two women's lives are identical, neither should their planners have to be! Your own notebook will become a lifesaving organizer, reminder, and reflection of your individual life routines, as mine has.

Keep your life message in focus, regardless of what chores seem to be beckoning.

Pray. Be sure to keep your life message in focus, regardless of what chores seem to be beckoning. Many things just don't need doing *today!* Rob's mother was a great housekeeper and taught me many wise housekeeping "tricks of the trade" during the years we lived near them in Florida. As a frustrated new mom, I wailed my woes to her about everything I thought needed attention. She helped me take a fresh look at my standards. They were too high.

"You don't have to have your kitchen floor clean enough for someone to eat off of. No one is going to!" That advice suited me and has greatly helped me keep perspective down through the years. It's okay to have toddler fingerprints on the sliding door, they can go nicely for weeks between cleaning. Likewise, having two daughters as apprentice homemakers has also served as a great means for delegation, thus lightening my load.

Enlisting Help When Drowning

I am thankful that Rob does not feel his masculinity is endangered nor his role of manliness threatened by helping with household responsibilities. Not long after we were married, we both fell naturally into performing certain tasks that suited us both. Our aim has always been to lighten each other's load, depending on the circumstances. When I was up during the night nursing babies, he handled a tremendous range of cooking, shopping, and cleaning.

Down through the years Rob would take the kids out somewhere in the evening just so I could have an hour or so to give the house a good once-over without interruptions.

As your children get older, make cleaning a family affair. Missy, Mindy, and I could do our heavy cleaning once a week and be done in half an hour. This was attainable because they each had a check list of light chores they needed to get done shortly after breakfast each morning. Because of this, housework did not consume all our time and energy. We started out years ago with those great chore charts from Current and they loved the accomplishment stickers. I've been in homes recently where they are hanging in full view like ours did from the refrigerator door.

There are numerous sources of affordable, available, outside help when needed. Call a high school or college-age student anxious to earn some extra cash. I cannot get through the holidays or heavily scheduled speaking engagement weeks without it! Form a co-op with friends or neighbors to trade jobs you detest or cannot physically do.

Turn the Tables

Maybe you would be willing to trade some baby-sitting for a friend's help on roofing or building a deck. A friend of mine does great wallpapering for trade-offs that benefit her. I enjoy splitting perennials in my garden and have even planted them in friends' yards in exchange for back-breaking jobs I cannot handle like painting or shampooing rugs.

Now that we're empty-nesting, rather than clean all on one day, Rob and I have a schedule of a few household chores that get done on certain days of the week. I know no one is going to come through giving a white glove test so I try to remind myself that *people are more important than things.* On crazy days when nothing gets done, I can at least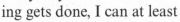

say to myself, "I threw in a load of whites today." I feel very strongly that it is better to spend a day with a hurting friend than it is to get certain chores done just because "it's my day to do them."

Good stewardship of our time often means delaying what can be done later. Chores are incidental to what's really important in our lives. One of my personal mentors the last few years, Florence Littauer, puts it well: "One of the quickest ways to gain perspective is to ask yourself, 'Is this going to make a difference two years down the line?' Inevitably, your answer will help clarify and redefine your priorities."

What is your perspective on scheduling? In her book, *Confessions of an Organized Housewife,* Deniece Schofield says, "You first decide how much time you can or want to spend cleaning."[6] It comes down to balance. I know when I'm focusing on all the responsibilities but not seeing the joys of life. My body always reminds me that I have been pushing too hard. A sore throat and severe case of sinusitis lets me know I need to remedy the burnout. There's only one way.

Mealtime Memories

You can build memories in your kitchen. Mealtime is traditionally a time for family to gather and share their lives together. You can instill the importance of making mealtime an opportunity for your family members to "connect," rather than hastily devouring unappealing, unplanned victuals on the run. Families' hectic schedules have almost made the "dinner hour" a thing of the past. The effort it takes to bring it back into your home is worth the effort! Expect some resistance from each family member when you unplug the phone, turn off the TV, and *sit* down together for the supper meal . . . as often as possible. Maybe you can't *every* night, but you could once a week.

A spirit of comfort is fostered when you set the stage with a creatively set table and healthy foods that are pleasing to the eye as well as the tastebuds. You will send a message by these gestures that heighten the anticipation of the meal. Any dish just tastes better when served in an attractive way. It also sends a message of care that you want mealtime to be a delicious time for the body *and* the soul.

I'm criss-crossing the country encouraging women to set aside one night as family night, especially at mealtime. As often as you can, share mealtime together as a family. Find what works for your household. Women who have embarked on this undertaking are reporting great improvements in communication and sharing in their families. I know it takes resolve, cooperation, and perhaps some juggling of schedules, especially if you have teenagers. But, you could try it once a week, if not every evening. The benefits and sweet memories are far-reaching! If you don't believe that, ask any lonely teen today. They will tell you they'd gladly give up anything (yes, even sports!) if they could have had close family ties and dinners together while growing up.

Many women now are sharing with me that in their own families, they've made suppertime a time of joyous sharing and family fun!

Bubbles, Bath, and Bible

Fifteen minutes a day scheduled in your daily planner *just for yourself* will help you renew emotionally, physically, and spiritually. One day I was able to pay a visit to a horse stable where some of the race horses were worth thousands of dollars. Their stalls were completely padded to guard against any infection from little scrapes and bumps. How much more should we as God's women guard our inner chambers! We can easily become bruised and scraped by this world's everyday problems. Renewing the soul keeps our inner self orderly and beautiful, whether the outer circumference is or not.

Happy is he that hath the God of Jacob for his help, whose hope is in the Lord his God.

(Ps. 146:5; KJV)

Honor yourself today with a time of sheer comfort. Find a relaxing treat that is low in fat content and high in inspirational value. It will put pep in your step! It could be a bathtub. It might be a lawn chair. Relax and read. The Bible is not only *for* you but *about* you. Let yourself imagine how God is comforting you. He is, with His dear nail-scarred hands.

When you want to feel anew . . . take some time for YOU! You can't have one without the other.

When There Aren't Enough Bathrooms in the House!

Whatever else might be said about home, it is the number one place I long to be when I have been on the road traveling for very long at all. Home. It's where I belong. Where comfort holds me in its warm embrace. No price tag can measure its value to me

and my family. I'm learning that it is not the comfort situations that bring out the depth of what home means to me, but often the difficult ones. B.J. Thomas belts out the lyrics to the song titled, "Home Where I Belong." You've heard it, and if you're of my generation, probably even sung along:

> When I'm feelin' lonely and when I'm feelin' blue,
> It's such a joy to know that I am only passin' through.
> I'm headed home. Goin' home, where I belong.

True, overall comfort reigns in our home. The last thing I want you to picture, however, is that ours is a Norman Rockwell picture-perfect family that has it "all-together." I don't think that even exists except in art! We, just like you and your family, occasionally get irritable, fall apart, and fail one another. Some days our home has been a great place to visit . . . but, I wouldn't want to live there.

Like when our house only had one bathroom, a mom, a dad, and two girls who were entering their teens. Every morning became an exercise in patience and endurance. Rob was patient and I endured. For an hour every morning and every night, I endured.

You see, living in a house with one bathroom really encouraged our "family togetherness." Or should I say, *discouraged* it. It seems that Missy absolutely *could not* brush her hair or teeth if Mindy was standing anywhere within 50 feet of her! No matter that the mirror extended the full length of the bathroom wall. The wailing and gnashing of teeth could be heard as far as the driveway.

"She's looking at me!" I recognized the voice as Missy.

"I am *not!* My eyes are straight ahead!" Mindy would retort back for whoever was listening. After repeated warnings and many frustrating mornings, a bathroom time schedule saved my sanity. I marvel now at how well both girls get along. I enjoyed hearing them giggle and gaggle while they were both home visiting for the holidays this year. They love to spend time together. Even in front of the same mirror!

We are constantly filing away at the rough edges. One thing I have learned over the years is that even with three bathrooms now, no home is ever going to be problem-free. There is no one-two-three, quickie formula for the questions homes are facing. During the tough times we will either grow stronger or grow apart.

Before You Blow Up in Anger

Sometimes sheer perseverance is all you might have going for you. Use it! Perseverance can be the mortar holding a home together when we allow walls to build up. Stress and anger are two of the most common "discomfort" walls. Both can be a double-edged sword. Both can be beneficial and can be destructive. They can prevent tragedy or cause travail. The first is usually a protective response, such as if you step into the path of an oncoming car. Stress and fear force you to jump out of the way, preventing disaster. Destruction comes if you allow the stress level to accumulate off the stress chart without intervening. Weigh the options.

Anger is often the result of stress overload. When I put too many plugs into my circuit breaker, there is overload

Cheerfulness keeps up a kind of daylight in the mind and fills it with a steady and perpetual serenity.

Joseph Addison (1672–1719)

and eventually, burnout. A total shut-down. If the system did not shut down, my house could catch on fire, causing total disaster.

As humans, we are much the same way. An overload of responsibilities and stress turns up the heat . . . boiling anger results.

Anger has become a way of life for many women, especially under the stress that parenting brings. Fears and concerns that moms 20 years ago did not even have to consider, now dominate daily thinking of mothers. Day care, guilt, kidnapping, deprived needs, abuse, resentments toward jobs or spouses, housekeeping needs . . . all can add up to intense discomfort.

These do not need to control you, however. The root is usually a displeasing situation that has made us bitter, resentful, or hostile — that's when it becomes anger.

Once you better understand the root of your anger, you can find practical ways to diffuse it. In "Steam Mad" by Jill Richardson[7] several ways include:

> **PLAN AHEAD:** Before conflict arises, talk with your children about the consequences of breaking rules.
>
> **BE REASONABLE:** Don't drag hungry, tired kids on a dozen errands. Recognize when you are demanding too much.
>
> **GET EVEN:** Don't yell about crackers on the carpet. Insist that the child clean up her own mess. Actions have consequences.
>
> **CHOOSE YOUR BATTLES:** Seat belts are non-negotiable. (So what if your preschooler wants to wear her swimsuit in the bathtub.)
>
> **STOP YELLING:** A parent's angry outburst can fuel a child's aggressiveness.
>
> **RESPOND IMMEDIATELY:** If you don't, the child will keep pushing the boundaries and then you'll explode. If you are boiling over, take five

and make your child do the same. Then deal calmly but firmly with the transgressor.

LIGHTEN UP: Start a whining contest with a fussy child. Tickle a complainer till he has to laugh! (I've tried this one and I love it!)

Those are terrific ways to control anger with children. There is an old Latin proverb, "He who goes angry to bed has the devil for a bedfellow." Yes, there are many irritations in life. But, "A fool gives full vent to his anger, but a wise man keeps himself under control" (Prov. 29:11).

Home Extension Rooms — The Garden

I love to sit on the deck just outside our back door that overlooks our backyard flower garden, the way I did just today. It is peaceful and serene, forcing me to write about the things God is doing in my life. On a post near the garden's entrance hangs a sign that reads "Love Grows Here." Pausing to ponder between paragraphs today, I realized what an impact that saying has.

No matter where I am or what I am, all that is required of me is to love. To be and do what I am supposed to be and do; but to always LOVE to the very best of my ability.

Today the late summer heat has made the leaves droop. Our scorching Iowa winds have blown over the tall, withering sunflower and hollyhock stalks. Without a drenching soon, they'll never make it.

I walk over to drag the hose in place. The cool nourishment soothes my soul as much as it revives the soil. My garden is an extension of our house — a room out of doors. It is perhaps my favorite room "in" our house. Maybe that's why I spend so much time there. In those quiet times I am free to withdraw from life's demands. In the silence of digging with a hoe or just wandering and listening . . . many of my dreams are born.

From Weeds to Wildflowers

My garden reaches far beyond the confines of its fragrant, colorful walls. That's the way a garden works! In 27 years of gardening, I have learned some healthy lessons there. I started out with six scrawny petunia plants around the tiny patio in our first apartment. Now, flower beds encircle our entire yard on all four sides. Lots of learning . . . lots of growing . . . lots of waiting.

In the classroom of my garden, I have learned a lot about my role as a mother. I'm to plant seeds in my daughters' lives. I then mulch, weed, water, and feed. Past that, the rest of their nurturing is up to God. With the most tender care and preparation on the part of parents, the time comes early when we must also begin to let go.

To plant a garden you can go to the garden center and buy two dozen tulip bulbs. You have prepared the bed removing obstacles that might obstruct growth. You place the bulbs in the soil bed. Cover and bed them down securely. Mulch. Feed. Weed. Water. WAIT. An entire season of waiting is important. Then and only then, do you reap a bountiful harvest.

Effective parenting follows the same sequence. There is no greater value in good parenting than the wisdom of waiting. Gardening helps us all to learn this patience. You just can't rush the growing process — in the garden or in your child's life. The tricky part is knowing how much fertilizer, digging, tending, and pruning to impose.

There is just no rushing flowers . . . or children. I once made the mistake of trying to force some garden blooms to open in time for a garden party. After a cool spring my roses, columbine, iris, and peonies were not at the stage I'd hoped they would be in time for our church Ladies Night Out group to gather on the lawn. I fertilized and watered. I pruned and prodded! To no avail . . . in spite of these extra efforts most buds had not had time to bloom. The results were out of my hands. Even with all this over-nourishing.

Similarly, I've been just as unfair with Missy and Mindy before. I've prodded, pushed, and prompted in times when what they have needed is my patience. Every child has his or her own individual time to bloom emotionally, as well as physically. There can be no comparing. No rushing. Each is one-of-a-kind with a timetable of her own! Beginning in toddlerhood, we parents need to gradually let our child make the transition from parental control to self-control. This gives a child the confidence and empowerment to enter teen years and adulthood.

I have watched the face of my friend Teresa's daughter light up in confidence when given the responsibility to make her own decisions. If little pre-schooler Ashlyn can only take one toy with her, Teresa says, "You decide." And Ashlyn does. She is being allowed to make a choice of her own and live with the consequences. Teresa is a terrific mother. What a wonderful way to teach responsibility at any age!

You just can't rush the growing process — in the garden or in your child's life.

Terrific But Specific

Florence Littauer, a dear friend and personal mentor of mine, has written a super book entitled *Silver Boxes*. She clearly shares how we all can be encouragers in positive speech to others. In her effervescent, practical style Florence shares that parents must be especially conscious to use words that build up and not tear down. "We must train ourselves to think before we speak. Once the words are out, we can't stuff them back in — they are intangible, illusive."[8]

Speech needs to be as Ephesians 4:29 tells us: "Do not let any unwholesome talk come out of your mouths, but only what is helpful for building others up according to their needs, that it may benefit those who listen." Wholesome speech encourages! Verse 32 goes on to say, "Be kind and compassionate to one another, forgiving each other, just as in Christ God forgave you."

Growing a Bumper Crop

In my garden I am the facilitator, the helper. God is the true gardener. It is because of His creativity and timing that I can triumphantly pick beautiful bouquets in bounty. As the parents of Missy and Mindy, Rob and I both acknowledge, "Every good and perfect gift is from above" (James 1:17). We dare not revel or take credit for their sweet lives. We may hold the trowel and shovel, but we know who is really behind their successes.

Your child has great worth and value. Let them know you feel that they do! I still remember a song named "Sugartime" we used to sing while riding the tractor on my grandparents' farm: "Sugar in the mornin', sugar in the evenin', sugar at suppertime. Be my little sugar and love me all the time!" We can take a lesson from this little jingle. May our words and actions be sweet!

Many authors have compared children to plants growing in the garden of life. Isn't it interesting today that gardeners talk to their plants and even leave music on in their homes to make them grow? If horticulturists talk to their plants to aid in healthy growth, how about trying it with your kids?

Sweetness . . . kindness . . . comfort . . . any time of the day!

How Do You Spell Love?

It takes time — lots of it — to cultivate a comforting climate in which children can grow. Resolve now to give the time your child needs, for "love" is actually spelled "T-I-M-E" to a child. Years ago I received a great garden tip from a seasoned gardener. He stressed to me the importance of checking my garden daily — first thing in the morning. That way, such problems as weed and pest invasions or dry areas can be spotted while they are still small and only take a small amount of time and effort to remedy.

It takes time — lots of it — to cultivate a comforting climate in which children can grow.

Just like my garden plants, it takes time DAILY to raise a healthy, happy child. In the morning, in the evening, suppertime . . . sugar all the time. Sugar for little tummies is discouraged. But, sweetness from a mother's heart is highly recommended!

IN THE MORNING: Henry Ward Beecher said, "The first hour of the morning is the rudder of the day." I go even further. I'm convinced that the first four minutes the family is together sets the tone for the day! Try to hug and hold — no matter how old your child is — your children in the morning. Even if it's a quick squeeze as they dash out the door.

Oh, yes, they will tell you that they've "outgrown that sort of thing." If you are not in the habit, they will pull away wailing, "Oh, Mom!" Then, about the third morning when you fail to hug or kiss them goodbye, they will seek YOU out first! Parents who withhold touch are not meeting a vital need and are depriving their children of the security of feeling wanted and loved. A girl, especially, will go looking for the stroking she needs, if she does not receive it at home.

Psychologists urge parents to keep on hugging, keep on roughhousing with their kids even into the teen years. They state the reason for rampant teen sex may not be that kids want a sexual relationship as much as they just need to be held.

One morning when the girls were still at home, I awoke exhausted from being up late the night before. I trudged into the kitchen and made coffee. Mindy padded in and watched me making my breakfast in my foggy state. I hadn't even acknowledged she was in the room. About to leave for work and tired of being ignored, she moaned, "Well, I guess I'm leaving now. . . ." She was hinting, something's missing! She knew I'd kiss and hug her goodbye and tell her I love her. Today, even though she's a grown woman, she still needs to be hugged and held.

IN THE AFTERNOON: Plants in my garden wilt in the hot afternoon sun of a summer day. They aren't very pretty or healthy-looking in that state. I don't go out there and start spading them all out of the ground tossing the plants onto the compost pile. I am confident that with some wise watering and "cooling off" time they'll burst forth again in full bloom.

A child needs to know he is not going to be yanked out of the garden and tossed aside when he wilts in the scorching heat of life. Love your sons and daughters unconditionally. Let them know you do. Not just when they are good. But, especially when they are not.

The story is told of a Mrs. Taylor's son who was arrested on a drug charge. The next day Mrs. Taylor put in for time off from work to accompany her son to court. An associate overheard her talking about the incident and remarked, "If he were my son, I'd kick him out!"

"If he were your son, I'd kick him out, too. But, he's not; he's mine," Mrs. Taylor shot back.

My daughters know that I'll never stop loving them — no matter what! Of course, I do not condone every decision they make or approve of everything they do. But, it doesn't affect my relationship with them. They know they aren't loved by what their actions are, but because of who they are. They are mine and Rob's daughters. We love them dearly . . . unconditionally. That holds us together when we become temporarily fragmented in stress or when distances separate us.

A child's feeling of worth is transmitted from his parents by acts of hugging, loving, praising, and accepting. Praise encourages and does wonders to help a child develop his or her special abilities.

A young woman tearfully told me, "My parents never said they loved me just because I'm me. I always had to do and be what they wanted. In fact, they even told me I was unwanted, a shameful "mistake." I have tried every way and every guy I know to find love."

How sad! Can you imagine what that did to her self-esteem? On the other hand, the mother who tells her child, "I believe in you. You can do it, I know you can!" conveys a message of love and confidence. If the youngster fails, he knows he is still loved. He dares to believe in himself. And that's a giant step for a little person to take!

I wonder many times that ever a child of God should have a sad heart, considering what the Lord is preparing for him.

Samuel Rutherford (1600–1661)

IN THE EVENING: Gardeners like my friends Carmen and Bruce, who have an acreage garden, don't just plant a seedling and forget it, hoping it will come up every spring with no maintenance. Even perennials take work. They have learned by experience how to prevent plants from wilting or weakening and how to rid them of disease and other problems. By evening there is a list of caring tasks still to be done.

Evening is an ideal time to spend loving your children. My girls used to enjoy the family bedtime rituals. "Who doesn't like delaying bedtime?" you say. I was always the one ready to hit the sack first since I'm more of a morning person. But, I am convinced that the energy and commitment it took to make bedtime memorable was *well worth it!*

What a better place this world would be if homes everywhere had parents who took time to read stories to their children at night, followed by a prayer together. Bedtime is a sweet memory time for our family. We all four reminisce about the rough-housing "rompie" times with Dad, quiet moments of sharing, and loving prayers that brought us all close together at the close of each day. That extra effort was well-invested for the girls and for me. Being a "hands-off" rather than a hands-on parent now, I hold those memories very dear to my heart.

Harvest Time

Gardening, like parenting, brings a lot of joy. It is also a lot of work. I must say, hard work in our garden has paid off. We save the tough jobs for when the sun goes down. Rob is gracious to do the heavy tilling job as I gradually am adding more beds each year. Umm . . . nothing like freshly tilled black dirt just waiting to be planted! I can hardly wait till he is done to get my hands in it!

My master gardener friend Carmen gave me another rule of thumb: work in plenty of compost and mulch whenever you put in a new plant. The little guy has to be able to breathe! And use chemicals sparingly and only as a last resort. Many insect infestations can be dealt with by just a strong blast of water from the hose.

I liken that advice to the way we are to both love and chasten our children. A gardener does not just plant seeds and let them be. Parents, don't just give birth and leave the rest to chance. Children are the product of many experiences, genetics, nutrition, and certainly of their parents' love. To see them blossom to their fullest, we must "work in" all the ingredients a new seedling needs to survive.

Nature tells us so. A plant can never be successful at extending its roots downward without preparing and softening the soil. Pushing deep into the ground, the well-rooted plant will be strong and anchored — no matter what storms may threaten!

Free to Stay Home

For a mom, no endeavor is more satisfying than the freedom to stay home or devote time to a career. For me, mothering full-time was completely my own choice. I was prepared to choose it joyfully, mindful that I was taking myself out of the professional writing and speaking arena for 20 years. I was confident that the 20 years in the "unpaid" work force at home would pay off in my daughters' lives. It certainly did. Without reservation, Rob supported me in that decision. We were single-minded in this concern for the welfare of our children.

Hopefully, you have reached your own answers to those compelling questions. They are difficult choices to make.

The energy and commitment it took to make bedtime memorable was well worth it.

I encourage you to *be there* during the season of your little ones' lives when they need the most nurturing and physical care. The first five years are especially critical.

Contrary to what some want us to believe, thousands of moms out there are nodding in complete agreement. I've met them all over this country! Don't miss out on your child's childhood just because some television documentary says it won't matter. Raising your child is a job that really matters — no matter *what* degrees you may hold. By being home you not only get to be there for your child's milestones, but you are there to kiss those hurts *when they happen, affirm their esteem, applaud their achievements, and help them in the way of the Lord on a daily basis.*

I used to balk at the question, "And what do you do?" Dear moms, never answer with *"Oh, I'm just a wife and mother."* Mothering at home may not stash a big bank account, but the dividends you are investing will be reaping interest far after you're gone. The media sometimes portrays full-time parenting as unflattering and demeaning.

But, the young mothers I meet all across the land are thankful every day for the joy they are allowed to fulfill as a full-time mother. They are not a bunch of crazed, right-wing, brain-dead women. These are talented, educated, creative women who are using their gifts to their fullest potential in their current profession of motherhood. It's a decision each woman must make for herself. I encourage you to think about it very seriously.

Many women return part-time to the work force out of financial necessity within a few years after childbirth. Some have found creative ways to supplement a second income in today's pressing economy. I applaud them! Have they lagged behind professionally? Perhaps a little, but they believe the tradeoffs have been well worth it.

It is impossible to over-estimate the value of a parent's love in a child's life. There is no adequate replacement. Children crave love much more than the lavish gifts any salary can provide.

In just six short months I will sit in the pew reserved for "mother of the bride." I'll watch with misty eyes as the young woman in white in the rear of the church confidently grasps her father's arm and glides forward. I will be suddenly aware of the brevity of motherhood. "They" were right all along, you know. I will join the ranks of "they" who counseled me, "Treasure every minute. You'll blink and she will be grown."

For 23 years I nurtured, educated, and prayed, and now am bringing in the harvest . . . all to raise a child who, as an adult, would follow the leading of her Lord. God entrusted Rob and me with a precious gift. I'm glad I set that phase of my life apart for mothering responsibilities.

No, I am not an extraordinary mother . . . I lose my patience, get frustrated, and still am not exactly clear on what a "good" mother is. But, somewhere amidst the diapers, dishes, and duties . . . God worked little miracles every day in the hearts of a little girl and young mother.

And on her wedding day, I will have good reason to be proud of the precious little girl who has now become God's woman.

Raising your child is a job that really matters.

PERSONAL OR GROUP STUDY GUIDE • WEEK 8

1. List the simplifying steps to the *Twenty-Five Thousand Plan:*

    1.

    2.

    3.

    4.

2. How can applying the $25,000 plan help you streamline your work and schedule?

3. Have you ever wondered why God does not take us straight up to heaven the moment we accept Him as Savior? We're called to serve Him here on this earth. Read Romans 12:1–2. Discuss how our lives and our bodies can be a "living sacrifice."

4. What gives your life great significance and value? When people think of "ministry" they often think of pastors or teachers. We are all called to be *servants* or *ministers.* When you serve others, you are serving God (Phil. 1:6; Eph. 4:13; 2 Cor. 3:18; 2 Tim. 3:14; Ps.102:18). One by one (or individually), share with the group how you plan to use your God-given abilities this week to be a *minister*, a servant for Christ.

5. How valuable is time to you? How are you going to be a better steward of time?

6. Are you putting your pursuit of earthly things ahead of what lasts or before your pursuit of God?

PRAYER PARAGRAPH:
Finish writing this paragraph prayer of service: Heavenly Father, the sad fact is that many of my days are spent not doing the things that really matter in light of eternity. Help me to schedule and prioritize better in the areas of _____

_____

_____

_____

                           Lovingly,
                           Your Daughter

Invite a Miracle Into Your Home

Rob and I sat in shock listening, yet not really grasping the full impact of the evening's news report. One of the local news reporters was standing in front of a house just minutes from ours. It was as if our minds refused to comprehend the horror. In disbelief, we caught bits and pieces of the story. All four residents were dead. During the night the father had violently shot and killed his son, daughter, and wife, then held the gun to his own head.

Rob and I sat speechless. We didn't know the family personally, but had shopped in their gift store and the couple had waited on me personally. Several of my friends knew them well and had worked side by side with them in various jobs over the years. What intense discomfort and pain was present in that home that could drive a father to think death was his only remedy?

Even more poignant to me than seeing the bodies being carried one by one out of the house, was the house itself. Television cameras panned in closely to capture ruffled curtains at each window, potted mums in bloom, and a fall holiday wreath on the door. Its architecturally elegant, yet relaxed design combined to create the seemingly perfect aesthetic setting. I'd been down that street many times. Even "garage saled" with a friend at that very house.

How "normal" the house had seemed. American suburbia. Now it had become a murder scene. A house of affluence

The accumulation of pleasures, possessions, and power does not make a house a home of comfort!

that looked quite content to the outside world had apparently been filled with some unseen resentment or smoldering anger for quite some time. I clipped the next morning's newspaper article for my journal. Its obvious message for me was loud and clear — the accumulation of pleasures, possessions, and power does not make a house a home of comfort!

Face it. You and I are afraid if we open the door of contentment, the unwanted guests of sacrifice and need will rush in. We've been led to believe that with the accumulating of "stuff" comes happiness. We're programmed to "get all you can" — whatever the sacrifice we have to make. We are made to feel ashamed if we don't keep up with the Joneses, or whatever names our neighbors might have.

Small wonder many of us stretch, strain, charge, and borrow in futile attempts to keep up a lifestyle that our culture claims is the "norm." Stop and think. Just about the time you think you have gotten all you need to be content, you begin to think you need something else. Or you observe that your friend has just gotten something better and bigger . . . whatever that "something" is . . . you fill in the blank!

We crave things that we don't need or enjoy. We buy things to impress others — people that we don't even know. Then we justify that we deserve something better. We must clearly understand that our insane attachment to possessions leads to feelings of inferiority and bondage. Not quite the life of comfort we'd like!

It took me a long time to learn to shout "No!" to indulgence. In my first year of marriage, I found myself in a shopping dilemma! Determined not to sacrifice my level of lifestyle, I opened my first credit card account. With those first purchases I felt so grown up! What a rush! I was in control! On my way to credit-card heaven!

The bill at the end of the month was a bit of a downer, but I didn't need to pay it all. I noted with growing interest (no pun intended) that the letter said I could finish paying next month. No big deal, then. Thoughts would cross my mind: *You can't afford this!* I would tell myself, *If one plastic brings this much ecstasy, how much can I enjoy with more cards?* Answer: Get more cards!

I spent more. Rob and I both spent more. We also fought and fretted more. Spending was in danger of becoming an addiction to replace the unhappiness and emptiness. It took more and more shopping sprees to provide the momentary feelings of power, control, and worth. There was always something new, something better out there to acquire. It was exhausting. All too soon, life came crashing down. We were deep in debt. We'd become enslaved to the things of this world.

I have learned, in whatsoever state I am, therewith to be content.

(Phil. 4:11)

That was over 25 years ago. I still remember how long it took to pay off all those bills. We began to be convicted about our spending. We drew up a rigid budget with the help of a financial counselor. For a long period of time we made up our own entertainment because we had no auxiliary spending. We learned what it was like to sit still before the Lord. We sought first the kingdom of God and his righteousness, and all the things that really mattered were added unto us (Matt. 6:33).

Life became simpler and far less complicated. All that "stuff" took too much time to care for anyway. We withdrew from the status race. One of the wonderful things about simplicity is its ability to give contentment in the gracious provision of God. No longer did we have a love affair going on with the accumulation of possessions.

Instead of walking through my home looking at things that could use replacing, refurbishing, or refinishing, I began to walk through my home praising and thanking God for having such a lovely shelter in which to live. Keeping my focus on the Lord rather than on stuff set me free! We were free from the bondage of this world's system and the "cravings of sinful man, the lust of his eyes and the boasting of what he has and does" (1 John 2:16).

If you find yourself discouraged and drowning in the stormy sea of financial debt, don't give up! At times, I make progress and then slip into old spending habits. That's a pattern for most of us in all areas of life, including finances. A correcting of our attitudes and actions keeps most of our desires in perspective. Remembering the stress and weariness that deep debt brought to my heart extinguishes the desire for foolish spending quicker than anything. "Better is little with the fear of the Lord than great wealth with turmoil" (Prov. 15:16).

That's the way it's got to be with you and me. When I really, really want something, God will give me the desire of my heart IF I "commit . . . to the Lord; trust in him" (Ps. 37:4–5). Notice the condition of committing and trusting. At times, the Lord allows me to have my heart's desires; other times He changes those desires. Still other times, He lets me wait and provides the financial means over time.

Whether in the state of wanting or the state of waiting, I can rejoice because I choose like Paul, "in whatsoever state I am, therewith to be content" (Phil. 4:11;KJV). Paul admits it's a learning process.

Listen to Jesus: ". . . be content with your pay" (Luke 3:14).

And to another apostle: ". . . not pursuing dishonest gain" (1 Tim. 3:8).

Now I warn you — it won't be easy. I don't mean to imply that at all. Contentment often requires marching out of step with others; being genuinely convinced that you are listening to the right drummer. That takes a miracle. It has nothing to do with the circumstances of life. It has everything to do with learning to trust a faithful God who can supply all your needs according to His riches in glory.

What comfort that kind of contentment can bring to your heart!

Do You Need a Miracle?

I have often found that I never truly appreciate something or someone until it is taken away, even if for a short time. Personal possessions, health, my children, emotional peace . . . expectations. Somehow, I have to admit, I thought I would be exempt from life's catastrophes. I guess I just assumed those were ugly realities that happened to everyone else. Not me.

Of course, I was wrong. Very wrong. Life is riddled with unexpecteds. Everyone wants to control their life. I used to think I could. With my day-timer and organizational skills in hand, I manage to control my life quite well, thank you. After all, aren't we told that the most successful and happiest people plot and plan?

A man travels the world over in search of what he needs and returns home to find it.

George Moore (1852–1933)

Sometimes it takes something like "the flood of '93" that deluged all of Des Moines. It was the most costly disaster in Iowan history. Thousands of homes were destroyed in the devastation. Plans and investments of many folks we know were reduced to rubble. I naively expected to come out of the experience unscathed. I expected to stay safe in my bed through the night. I expected to keep all my possessions. I expected to glide above troubled waters.

My expectations failed. Water swallowed the entire downstairs of our home. My treasure became trash. Over the rest of the summer my schedule was altered. Even the simplest of plans were affected without water, gas, or electricity and the time it took in long water lines those first weeks. Instead of being in control, I found myself groping for flashlights and buckets in the dark, learning firsthand what being "not in control" really means.

Control is a big issue for all of us. Being in control means that life would live up to my expectations. I'll be the first to admit this is a big issue for me. Attempting to control our own life (and others') is a trap we women fall into often, whether consciously or unconsciously. After all, when we're in control — kids obey, husbands are loving, and friends are supportive. Everyone jumps through our hoops. Right?

Not always so. No matter how well we manipulate to get control of our lives, those unexpecteds are going to come. Flood waters of frustration, helplessness, anger, and despair rush in at any moment. How strongly do you try to control your life? As a wife, do you manipulate using food, whining, sex, or guilt to control your husband? Do you use screaming, affection, and bribes to control your children and friends?

Are you experiencing a fearful flood right now? Perhaps you have just about drowned. You question if your life will ever seem "normal" again. You may be wondering if you are even going to survive — you're not so sure you even want to.

Is God still in the miracle-working business? You betcha! He alone is the sure Rock on whom we can stand when the floods of life come pouring in over life's shifting sands. We can sing, "On Christ the solid Rock I stand. All other ground is sinking sand." We can say with the Psalmist:

> God is our refuge and strength, an ever-present help in trouble. Therefore we will not fear, though the earth give way and the mountains fall into the heart of the sea, though its waters roar and foam and the mountains quake with their surging (Ps. 46:1–3).

It took me a while to understand, but I found Isaiah 43:2–3 to be a great comfort during the flooding:

> When you pass through the waters, I will be with you; and when you pass through the rivers, they will not sweep over you. . . . For I am the Lord your God.

Many homes and many lives badly need a miracle. Right now. Today. Let me show you what I've learned about miracles during another time of personal desperation. This time the only flood waters streaming were my tears. I came to realize my absolute inability to do anything and God's ability to do the miraculous.

He is the happiest, be he king or peasant, who finds peace in his home.

Johann Wolfgang Von Goethe (1749–1832)

Crash Landings

Unwittingly, I had assumed that since we raised our daughters in a godly home we would never face one of them straying spiritually. When I saw other parents and their children struggling, I'd wonder what those parents had done wrong. Now I view other parents and their children with compassion rather than judgment.

I rocked both of my daughters as infants, played hide and seek with them as toddlers, and walked them right up to the classroom door on their first day of school. For hours I sat on hard bleachers watching ball games, cheerleading, and school plays. I agonized over algebra and dating disappointments. I was there for the big moments, as well as the everyday, mundane moments. I invested so much providing the best protection, support, and love that I could.

And then I found out, I had to let them go! Release them! Cut the strings!

Off to college Missy and Mindy both flew — over a thousand miles away. When the fledgling, almost-adult child flies that far from the nest, it's inevitable that there will be some false starts — or some crash landings. It's all a part of testing their wings.

Our family survived the loneliness that first year the girls were gone. Rob and I grieved the part of our life that was over. After a couple of months we truly began enjoying our newfound relationship. Our empty nest was quickly turning into a love nest.

With the door of a whole new world opened up to her for the first time, Mindy reveled in being so far from home and parental authority. She had always been so strong in her love for God, that I was not worried. That is, at first.

I could tell within the first week of her junior year, Mindy was hurting. Over the phone the pain came through little by little even though she tried to cover it up with cheery bits of news and small talk. As we picked her up at the airport for Christmas break, my worst fears were confirmed. One look into her eyes told me what I'd only suspected and could not see through the phone wires.

A mama can see it in her own child's eyes. I couldn't miss the pain I saw. Mindy was a wounded, hurting young woman. Oh, how my heart ached for my daughter. I did not know what she had been through or where the pain was coming from, but the girl I took home from the airport that day was not the same girl I had seen take off five months before.

Where Do You Take Broken Dreams?

I began to do what any loving mom would do. I prodded; I preached; I pleaded. That did a lot of good. Yeah, right.

I cried through much of the holidays. One day, looking for Christmas presents, I had to leave the store when Mindy came to mind. It was difficult for me to see her getting hard and hateful at times. She had always been such a sensitive, loving person. The more I saw Mindy hurting, the more I hurt. I did not know how to help or get her to open up. I felt squarely up against the one situation over which I had no answers and no control.

New Year's Day arrived with a bang — literally! Jolting me out of my journaling was the ring of our telephone. It sounded like a gun shot — and the message on the other end had an effect on me nearly as powerful. The voice on the other end identified himself as our local police. I had never received a call prefaced with that statement. (That's the call other parents get; so I thought.) He began with a question about an incident involving some young people on New Year's Eve. Our Mindy included.

A palace without affection is a poor hovel, and the meanest hut with love in it is a palace for the soul.

Robert Green Ingersoll (1833–1899)

My heart sank. When confronted the previous night she had reported having a "boring, quiet evening." What I was hearing from the officer did not sound either quiet or boring!

I tried to finish my coffee and goal-setting and re-committing, which was my custom on every other New Year's Day. I usually loved that yearly "clean slate," but on this New Year's morning, pain paralyzed me. No goal-setting for the year appeared on the blank paper before me. Only questions stared back.

What did I do wrong as a mom to make Mindy deliberately choose to walk down such a destructive road? Had I been too strict . . . too easygoing . . . expected too much . . . too little? How could a woman who goes all over the world teaching other women have an adult child living a lifestyle that does not affirm her teachings? Blaming myself had a way of trapping me in a rut that dug me deeper into a hole of despair.

During the next weeks my faith roller-coastered. Even as I comforted myself with the many times I had seen God answer prayer, I struggled under the horrendous doubts that He would do it again. I scoured my Bible for a promise to claim that could give me hope.

I came across the stories in the Bible where other parents were in need of a miracle for their child (Matt. 17, Mark 7, Luke 8, Mark 9). They all did the same thing. They ran to Jesus for help. Sometimes He healed immediately; other times the miracle was delayed. Jairus pleaded with Jesus to heal his daughter. The bystanders laughed at his pleas and said she was already dead. No use to trouble Jesus now. Jesus answered them that she was not dead, only sleeping.

That's it! Mindy's not gone yet! There's still hope! She's just asleep! Asleep to the truths that haven't awakened in her heart yet!

One evening, Rob and I thought it might be a safe time to bring up our thoughts to Mindy. Boy, were we wrong! We tried to be kind and loving. Unwittingly, our words sounded self-righteous and judgmental. Alienated further, Mindy walked out during supper in a restaurant. For 40 minutes I walked the mall searching in every shop for my daughter. Tears streaming down my face, I didn't care who I ran into. I just wanted to find Mindy. I wasn't sure if or when I'd ever see her again.

Finally, I spotted her at the mall entrance. No, she did not want a ride home. Yes, she had already called someone to come get her.

I fully expected to find her room cleared out when we arrived home. Rob caught up with me carrying the uneaten dinners in to-go boxes. We headed home to see what we'd find. Or not find.

Not knowing when (or if) Mindy was returning, I knelt beside the bed in her room to pray. It was all I knew to do. I could not carry my pain anymore. Sobbing, I buried my head in Mindy's pillow. I remember smelling her sweet scent and hugging that pillow like I longed to hug her.

With God in charge, our weaknesses can enable His strength to flow through.

I wanted a miracle just like the parents I had read about in the Bible. I knew I had to do what they did. Go straight to Jesus. That is just what I did. Like Jairus, I "fell at Jesus' feet, pleading with him to come to his house because his only daughter, a girl of about twelve, was dying" (Luke 8:41). Even when others thought the girl was too far gone and they "laughed him to scorn," Jairus kept pleading with Jesus to raise up his daughter.

I did the same. I didn't know what else to do. I began by giving Him my fears, my pain, and my sorrow. As if they were a present, I verbally laid down my broken dreams and the expectations that I had for Mindy. Visually I wrapped them in beautiful paper and put a bow on top!

"Lord, she's yours, not mine," I prayed. "I fear the dangers of her lifestyle and what might happen, but she belongs to you. Not to me. You can take Mindy and do what You see best. I won't fight against You anymore. Please take hold of her hand like you did Jairus's and say, 'Arise.' Please revive Mindy, too!"

New Beginning

O God,
What shall I do?
I am at the total end
Of myself.
Wonderful, dear child!
Now start your new beginning
With me.
— Ruth Harms Calkin[9]

Comfort Comes Softly

Having given such a great sacrificial gift, I expected to feel sad and fearful of what might happen next. Instead, I felt lighter, happier than at any time since Mindy's return home. I had admitted the possibility of what I feared most. I had walked right up to my fear.

And the result? The result was surprising: my fear was gone. By releasing Mindy to God, I released myself from responsibility. What happened to Mindy now was up to God.

Matthew 17 teaches that the faith for such a miracle cannot happen "but by prayer and fasting." Rob and I implored our immediate extended family to devote one day where Mindy would be prayed for during the next few months. We knew this was a critical time.

Every one of us emerged better, not bitter, from those months. God's intention through all that was to drive us closer to himself, not farther from himself. I began to realize that God was working all things for my good, regardless of the outcome on Mindy's part. That was up to God.

One morning when Mindy got called in to work, I went to the counseling session in her place. (I knew we'd have to pay the fee for canceling too late anyway, so I figured it couldn't hurt.) His advice was like soft snow — it fell on my heart softly and sank in deeply. I was told just what I needed to hear. "Sharon, you are not responsible for Mindy's decisions. You are not the cause for what is going on right now, and you are not the cure."

That was good for me to hear. I was encouraged to keep loving and affirming to Mindy. So I did. Often a difficult task — especially on those days when I didn't feel like liking her, let alone loving her. I came to grips with the mistakes I made as a parent and sought Mindy's forgiveness. I found out that the words "I'm sorry" don't make a person choke after all. She graciously listened and forgave.

And these words . . . shall be in thine heart: And thou shalt teach them diligently unto thy children.

(Deut. 6:6–7; KJV)

Softly, silently, God's comfort filled our home again. We did what Lamentations 2:19 says to do: "Pour out your heart like water in the presence of the Lord. Lift up your hands to him for the lives of your children."

We were encouraged from Scripture, expecting great things to happen. Those "things" didn't happen all at once. But, I began to realize our home was once again filled with an atmosphere of love and understanding. And even fun some days!

I learned to allow God to work in His timing. While waiting on Him, the Lord showed me that the attitudes I was allowing in my heart were as sinful as my daughter's rebellion. That broke me. All I could do was confess them, weep over them, and plead with God for cleansing and mercy. I stopped lecturing and criticizing her. Most importantly, I prayed and loved her. The miracle of comfort followed.

Oops! Too Much Lotion!

By taking off our guarded, concrete masks, all of us — Sharon, Rob, and Mindy began to release a smile or two. One day we got downright fanatical and laughed a big belly laugh over something silly at the supper table! That night I recorded the event in my journal! It was as if Jesus himself was infusing us with a sense of hope. "Relax!" He seemed to say lovingly, "There's not a thing wrong here that I can't take care of."

A few weeks after the restaurant incident, while I was rinsing the dishes one evening, Mindy came through the kitchen to chat. When I was done I dried my hands and poured out hand lotion. Way too much hand lotion. I held out my hand to see if Mindy wanted the excess. I will never forget those moments that followed.

I took her hands gently into mine and caressed them as if they were the soft fur of a kitten. For at least 30 seconds we soothed lotion into one another's hands.

In those tender moments, looking eyeball to eyeball at one another, we shared much more than hand lotion that day. It was a real turning point. In that simple gesture of only a few moments, it was as though the soothing balm of Gilead was being applied to our souls (Jer. 8). Not only our hands, but both of our hearts were soothed and softened.

God is able to heal hurts. Out of our admitted weaknesses — physical, mental, emotional, spiritual — can come His marvelous strength. Instead of our weakness being a hindrance, with God in charge, our weaknesses can enable His strength to flow through.

Any time our family uses hand lotion now, we always pour out a little extra. We turn to the nearest person and share! Even my mega mass of a husband! Rob used to think lotions were too "girly and gooey." He even likes to get in on the group lotion lovin' now!

With God in charge, our weaknesses can enable His strength to flow through.

Want, Waive, Wait, Watch!

From the vantage point of nearly two years later, I can see how I was being forced to lie in green pastures by very still waters. When God wants to get your attention — He does it through those you love the most. In those pastures I:

WANTED A MIRACLE
WAIVED (RELINQUISHED) ALL RIGHTS
    AND ALL CONTROL
WAITED FOR A MIRACLE. God's timing
    is always best!
WATCHED GOD WORK!

Today Mindy is doing just fine. She is *so much more* than just fine! She's awesome! Serving on the staff of a great church for six months now, she is looking forward to starting work on her master's in counseling soon. God has done exceedingly abundantly more than I ever dared dream!

Do you need a miracle in your home? Maybe it isn't concerning a son or daughter. Maybe it concerns health, husband, finances, attitudes, betrayal, loss . . . whatever despair you are facing. Don't give up hope! Whenever you say something is hopeless, you slam shut the door of God working a miracle. Let me encourage you to get back on the path of hope today!

And don't forget to stock up on some hand lotion. You're gonna need it!

PERSONAL OF GROUP STUDY GUIDE • WEEK 9

1. How does creating a warm and caring environment in my home make the high calling of motherhood "the toughest job you'll ever love"? What are some ways we can lead children in "ways everlasting" to mold and shape their little lives in a hectic world?

2. What major differences are there between mothers who raise their children in the things of God and those who don't? Read 2 Chronicles 22:2–4; 2 Timothy 1:5–6; 3:14–15.

3. How do mothers manipulate and control their children (of any age)?

4. These parents knew where to run when they needed a miracle with their child. Do you? See Matthew 17, Mark 7, Luke 8, and Mark 9.

5. Have others ever told you that your child was "too far" gone or that you'd "might as well give up" like Jairus was told. Did your faith waver? Did you give up? Have you given your child totally to God and acknowledged that he or she is only "loaned" to you?

6. What can you do while waiting for your miracle in your home (Is. 40:31; Ps. 57:1)? (See also Matt. 17— it teaches the discipline of prayer and fasting when seeking a miracle for a child).

7. What is the most vital responsibilities upon a mother when God entrusts her with a child? Think of how you could be a better parent to your children.

PRAYER PARAGRAPH:
Finish writing this prayer paragraph of relinquishment: Lord, I pray that I will understand how to parent properly from Your example of how You parent me as Your child. I pray I will not be critical, cold, or cruel, but rather _____
_____
_____
_____

Lovingly,
Your Daughter

Conclusion

Fastened just above my kitchen sink are two identical switches. One turns on an overhead light, the other discharges the garbage disposal. While putting together a meal or cleaning up afterwards, I often spin around quickly and flip a switch. What follows, more often than not, is an ear-piercing rumble signaling me that my hand truly is quicker than my eye. Everything from glass candleholders to a dog collar has been caught in the grip of that disposal to meet a perilous fate.

Oh sure, my intentions are good. But, blame it on haste, preoccupation, stress, or the sheer fact that I'm blonde . . . inevitably, when I want to turn on the light, up goes the switch to the disposal. (I have several earrings that have chewed-up mates!)

I think we are just like that in our homes sometimes. Though our intentions start out good, we're on overload or too preoccupied, busy, or stressed out to take notice of what we're reaching for or whose buttons we're pushing. Hurling through depression, divorce, discouragement, disagreements, or death (all of which could hit our homes at one time or another), we find ourselves mutilating the feelings of those we love the most. First, our teeth clamp down hard on anyone who gets in the way. Then, click! On goes the button that sucks in, chews up, and noisily disposes of the precious ones we love.

Like garbage.

All that's left behind is an empty vacuum in a heart. Frightening, isn't it? That scenario does not describe at all how I used to play house as a little girl. I loved to dress up in fancy, oversized clothes and gather my dolls together, all lined up as a family. Using old pie tins and Velveeta boxes, I'd cook on miniature stoves with play dishes. My playmates and I would enjoy endless hours of this happy pretend play. After it would get late or we'd get hungry or fussy, I'd take my dolls and go home. Game over.

Constructing a home of comfort isn't over when the fun and games end. It is day-in and day-out overtime. Dear friend, God has the best blueprint. He is knocking at your heart's door and He's laid out the welcome mat. Just for you. God alone can secure the walls of your home so that it can withstand even the fiercest of storms. I've taken you on a tour through the rooms of my home and introduced you to my loved ones who have lived in those rooms. The storms of discomfort huffed and puffed and all but blew our house down . . . but, through Christ, it still stands.

No matter what sin or pain might be in your home from the past, Jesus is ready to forgive, to heal, and to comfort. Let Christ become the titleholder of your home — and yes, of your heart. Let Him in. Drop the key at His feet in surrender, praying, "Not my will, but Thine be done." A deep peace will settle under your roof. I can give you my word, there is no better home in which to live. In fresh, unimaginably marvelous ways He will be there with happiness, hope, and harmony. to fill your heart when you truly *come home to comfort.*

Endnotes

1 *Daily Bread*, Radio Bible Class Ministries, Grand Rapids, MI.
2 Erich Fromm, *The Art of Loving* (New York, NY: Harper and Row Publishers, 1974).
3 Marjorie Holmes, *As Tall as My Heart* (McLean, VA: EPM Publications, distributed by Hawthrone, 1974).
4 Gary Smalley, *Love Languages* (Chicago, IL: Northfield Publishing, 1992).
5 F.J. Wiens, *Her Best for the Master* (Chicago, IL: Moody Press, 1964).
6 Deniece Schofield, *Confessions of an Organized Housewife* (Cincinnati, OH: Better Way Books (Div. of F & W Publishing, Inc., 1994).
7 Jill Richardson, "Steam Mad," *Christian Parenting Today*, Sept.–Oct. 1996, Vol. 9, No. 1, p. 26–28.
8 Florence Littauer, *Silver Boxes* (Dallas, TX: Word Pub., 1994), p. 30, "The Gift of Encouraging Words."
9 Ruth Harms Calkin, *Lord, It Keeps Happening and Happening* (Wheaton, IL: Tyndale House Publishers, 1983).